Tom Lucan
1989
Berkeley

LISP
THE LANGUAGE OF
ARTIFICIAL INTELLIGENCE

No. 2620
$25.95

LISP
THE LANGUAGE OF
ARTIFICIAL INTELLIGENCE

FREDERICK HOLTZ

TAB BOOKS Inc.
Blue Ridge Summit, PA 17214

TAB BOOKS Inc. offers software for
sale. For information and a catalog,
please contact TAB Software
Department, Blue Ridge Summit,
PA 17294-0850.

FIRST EDITION

FIRST PRINTING

Library of Congress Cataloging in Publication Data

Holtz, Frederick.
    LISP, the language of artificial intelligence.

    Includes index.
    1. Artificial intelligence—Data processing.
2. LISP (Computer program language) I. Title.
Q336.H65 1985   006.3   85-22233
ISBN 0-8306-0420-0
ISBN 0-8306-0320-4 (pbk.)

Contents

Introduction

LISP is the language most associated with artificial intelligence (AI), the field in which computers are programmed to react in a human-like manner.

LISP (the acronym stands for LISt-Processing language), was only recently implemented on personal computers. Prior to this, it was used by scientists and was run on multimillion dollar mainframes. Only mainframes had the power to make full use of LISP.

Some LISP systems became available for microcomputers shortly after the IBM PC was introduced. Unfortunately, many microcomputer implementations of LISP were quite limited and were often crude subsets of the full LISP language. Then too, there were many different versions or dialects of LISP, including MacLISP, ZetaLISP, Spice LISP, and others.

The microcomputers of the first part of this decade were limited in addressable memory, speed, and many other factors essential to LISP. No serious attempts were made to produce a microcomputer implementation that could be used as an artificial intelligence development tool.

Microcomputers are now far more powerful. RAM, which was very expensive a few years ago, is now cheap. The days of the 16K computer are gone for good. While 64K of RAM used to be considered pretentious for a microcomputer, most machines now come equipped with a minimum of 256K and some may contain a megabyte or more. It soon became apparent to a few companies dealing in LISP that the microcomputer was now mature enough to accept LISP development packages.

The multidialect barrier was hurdled by the recent development of Common LISP, a collection of all those other dialects and more. Common LISP was designed to become the industry standard and it is gaining wide reception.

Common LISP is available in powerful implementations for microcomputers. This book is an introduction to Common LISP and it is specifically aimed at BASIC programmers with little or no experience in other languages.

There are many, many books on LISP available. The number of Common LISP books is far smaller, but it is growing. However, most Common LISP books are not aimed at the BASIC programmer. BASIC is an excellent language, but it does not directly prepare its users to grasp the concepts of other languages. Therefore, the transition from BASIC to other high-level languages is usually difficult.

It is hoped that this book will not only introduce you to Common LISP in a simple and understandable manner, but that it will make other Common LISP books more useful by building a firm knowledge of LISP fundamentals in the minds of BASIC programmers.

This book should not be thought of as a reference source of Common LISP. Instead of discussing and explaining every facet of LISP in detail, this book selects major elements of Common LISP and fully explores each; it even shows how BASIC programs can be rewritten in Common LISP using these major elements.

This book takes what is essential to understanding LISP and presents it in such a way that you can build from your knowledge of LISP fundamentals.

This book won't make you a LISP expert. That will take many more hours of study, not to mention the time required to understand artificial intelligence applications. This book does teach you the LISP fundamentals and allows you to go as far as you desire.

Artificial intelligence is not the wave of the future; it is the wave of the present. By gaining an understanding of LISP, you will be able to enter this area with confidence.

Chapter 1

LISP: A
List-Processing Language

LISP is currently the most popular and best-known language used in the development of computer programs that seem to emulate human thought processes. Artificial intelligence was and still is a highly controversial area of computer programming. There are many views on just what artificial intelligence really is. This is not surprising since there are equally many arguments over the nature of human intelligence really is, as well as the actual makeup of the human thinking process.

When discussing artificial intelligence, terms such as *heuristics, machine intelligence,* and *cognitive manipulation* often crop up. Generally, *artificial intelligence* is the ability of a device (a computer) to adapt to new situations, to distinguish fact from fiction, to improve its level of performance based upon experience, and to learn.

This might be taken to mean that the ultimate operation of the artificially intelligent machine is equal to more than its initial programming. We might also say that a machine that exhibits artificial intelligence is able to learn from its mistakes and not repeat those mistakes.

The arguments on how to develop artificial intelligence have placed their practitioners in two basic categories. One group thinks that artificial intelligence can best be accomplished by the "engineering approach." This is an effort to create a system that is capable of dealing with problems or tasks using methods suited to a machine or computer, as opposed to simulating the processes a human might use. The engineering approach involves such things as pattern matching, recognition of objects or people, and text/music composition. To many this is not true artificial intelligence because it addresses a very limited area. While it is true that humans can recognize patterns, compose music, and write text, the accomplishment of these tasks by a machine is not enough in itself, at least according to the other major group in the artificial intelligence field.

This second group lauds the "modeling approach" to artificial intelligence. Machines that fall into this category attempt to mimic the human thinking processes in order to perform a task. An AI computer would go through the steps a human would in identifying, reasoning through and completing a task. Of course, the modeling approach group is split into many subcategories based on disagreements over just what the human approach is.

The modeling approach often depends more on heuristics than on algorithms. A *heuristic* is best described as a "general procedure" or, more appropriately, a "loose rule of thumb" for a task. One crude example of a heuristic is what to do if you're attacked by an African lion. The general rule of thumb would dictate that you run away from the lion. There is no way that this can be converted to an algorithm because there are too many variables. If you had a gun in your hand, then the best solution might be to shoot the lion. But this might apply only if you knew you could not run to safety.

Sometimes we humans do not have the time or ability to completely think through a stressful situation. In these cases we often rely on hunches or intuition. There are those who feel that hunches are merely loose collections of rules of thumb garnered through experience. This means that a hunch is a rapidly-thought-out procedure based upon accumulated data. Some even hold that many hunches are as accurate as a carefully thought out procedure and that both involve the same collection of data.

Of the two groups of artificial intelligence researchers mentioned, the "engineering method" group thinks it is best to get the job done, regardless of the method used to accomplish it. The "modeling approach" group thinks that it is imperative to get the job done by going through the same basic thinking processes a human would. While both groups make good points, the first machines that border on artificial intelligence will probably be a combination of both research directions.

WHAT IS COMMON LISP?

LISP is an acronym for *list processing*. Obviously, it is a list-processing algorithm that can be defined as a computer language that facilitates the processing of data presented in list form, as opposed to individual elements or objects. LISP was originally developed at MIT by John McCarthy and his associates in the late 1950s and 1960s. LISP is often called a "process-description language." It is highly useful in the field of artificial intelligence because it is precise, easy to learn, and unambiguous.

Since its development, many dialects of LISP have cropped up, presenting compatibility problems. This has also made transporting LISP programs from one computer to another quite difficult. This book describes Common LISP, the newest dialect of LISP. Common LISP is recognized as a successor to MacLISP, which sprung out of ZetaLISP and Interlisp. This parallels what happened to BASIC after it was developed at Dartmouth College. While Microsoft BASIC (MBASIC or MS-BASIC) is the standard for microcomputers today, just a few years ago there were many different versions. All had similarities, but all had differences.

In 1982, the Defense Advanced Research Projects Agency (DARPA) encouraged a group of world-class programming language experts to design Common LISP. This was done in an attempt to consolidate the many dialects and splinter dialects that had developed from the original LISP. LISP had grown into a language that offered universal acceptance and was evolving into an industry-supported standard.

The Common LISP design consortium included experts from Bell Laboratories (responsible for the C programming language, UNIX operating system, etc.), Carnegie-Mellon University, Digital Equipment Corporation, Hewlett-Packard Corporation, Lawrence Livermore Laboratory, LISP Machines, Inc., MIT, Perq Systems Corporation, Symbolics, Inc., Tartan Laboratories, Inc., Texas Instruments, Inc., University of California at Berkeley, University of Utah, Xerox Corporation, and Yale University.

This prestigious list of companies, laboratories, and universities called the end product of their research Common LISP—an appropriate name, since it incorporates all that is good (arguably) from the other dialects. The result is a LISP version that is quickly being recognized and as a adopted common element in diverse LISP programming endeavors.

Companies with current Common LISP implementations include Data General Corporation, Digital Equipment Corporation, Gold Hill Computers, Symbolics, Inc., and Texas Instruments, Inc. This list is growing, and it seems that Common LISP will soon be the industry standard.

As the research model for this book, I chose the Golden Common LISP programming package from Gold Hill Computers, in Cambridge, Massachusetts. According to their literature, Gold Hill's prime objective is advanced research into artificial intelligence for industry in order to meet the increasing demand for more intelligent software.

Because of fairly recent technological advances in the field of microcomputers, it is now possible to bring artificial intelligence problem-solving techniques to the personal computer. Golden Common LISP is the first Common LISP implementation for the IBM Personal Computer (PC) and 100 percent IBM-compatible machines. Gold Hill Computers is also developing powerful artificial intelligence applications for the office marketplace.

I chose Gold Hill's implementation partly because it was good for the LISP beginner and also because this company uses LISP as its core technology. They note that since LISP's development some 25 years ago, it has evolved into a modern, general-purpose language, applicable to many different applications and fields. It is associated with high programmer productivity because of its powerful primitives and extraordinary development environments.

Until recently, LISP existed only on expensive mainframes and special-purpose LISP machines. Today's personal computers are powerful enough to support LISP systems, creating an opportunity to lower the cost of learning, using, and delivering LISP and LISP-related applications.

Golden Common LISP is an extended subset of Common LISP for the personal computer. After extensive development and user testing, Golden Common LISP was released by Gold Hill Computers in November 1984. The version used as a model for this book (version 1.01) was released in mid-1985 and is a slight update of the original. It contains the GCLISP interpreter, the GMACS editor, an EMACS-like full-screen editor, the San Marco LISP Explorer (an interactive tutorial), the GCLISP On-Line Help System, and two LISP reference books.

LISP programming packages designed for microcomputers are usually accompanied by an on-screen tutorial, but the San Marco LISP Explorer is more than a tutorial. It is nothing short of excellent. With this tutorial, the newcomer who is familiar with BASIC or some other computer language should quickly become comfortable with Common LISP. The Golden Common LISP manual is a very thorough (though dry) reference source that will look like Greek to the beginner. After spending a week or two with the San Marco LISP Explorer, however, this reference source becomes far more valuable.

I did say a week or two when referring to the tutorial. It is long, thorough, and sometimes exhausting, but it does cover all the materials needed to become well versed in Common LISP. The San Marco teaching method allows the student to leave the tutorial at any time to practice what has been learned. This is done under the Golden Common LISP interpreter. Reentering the tutorial environment is as easy as leaving it.

I mentioned that LISP on microcomputers has been a fairly recent development. There have been LISP microcomputer implementations available for several years, but most of these could hardly be called true development packages. These served their purpose by teaching LISP and allowing the user to become comfortable in a LISP programming environment. However, many were just not adequate for serious development work.

Golden Common LISP is a true LISP development package. It allows the beginner to quickly learn Common LISP and then to move on to development work. It does not limit the user through an inability to address all of the RAM available as do some LISP packages. It offers a comprehensive set of development tools not often seen in a microcomputer LISP environment (such as a full-screen editor). I think of it as a professional development package that offers the beginner the tools to learn the trade. You can also expand it as you upgrade your computer.

For someone who just wants to play around with LISP, Golden Common LISP is probably not the thing. First of all, it's priced to avoid that. Retailing at $495, it hardly fits the financial range of "just foolin' around" software. Nor will you be able to implement GCLISP on a bare-bones IBM PC. You will need a PC, PC-XT, PC-AT, or 100 percent PC-compatible machine with at least 512K memory. You can use this package with a single 5 1/4-inch floppy disk drive, but you should have at least two disk drives. Ideally, you should have a hard disk rated at 10 megabytes or more. This makes installation a lot quicker and the system will operate faster because of the decreased read/write times.

GCLISP will also support the Mouse Systems PC Mouse, an Intel 8087 Math Coprocessor, and either the monochrome or color graphics display boards. Gold Hill Computers stresses that all hard disks, diskette drives, drive controllers, and display adapters must be IBM or IBM-compatible. I have tested this package with the Amdek MAI color/monochrome adapter board and with Quadram Quaddisk 27 megabyte hard disk drives and controllers and experienced no compatibility problems. I have also used GCLISP with the Quadram Sprint processor board, which effectively doubles the speed of the IBM PC. Again, there were no compatibility problems.

The GCLISP Interpreter

The GCLISP Interpreter contains an extended subset of Common LISP. This means that it contains many of the primitives and capabilities of the complete Common LISP language, but not all of them. "Extended subset" also means that the Common LISP attributes that have been included have been augmented by variations designed to make programming the supported computer (the IBM PC) easier. GCLISP contains some graphics primitives not native to Common LISP that address the IBM PC specifically.

These are a part of that extension.

CGLISP contains advanced data types such as closures, stack groups, vectors, named structures, and single-and double-precision floating-point numbers. It also includes a set of modular programming primitives such as SETF, IF-THEN-ELSE, CASE, DO, CATCH/THROW, DO-LIST, and UNWIND-PROTECT.

Another very important feature for the serious developer are the coroutines that allow multitasking operations. The ability to use macros provides much greater code clarity and saves programming time. Subprimitives such as %DRAW-LINE and %FILL support color graphics operations, and GCLISP offers full DOS support, including random file access. The user can enter and exit the DOS environment from within the GCLISP environment.

Streams are used for all input and output, allowing easy redirection. For example, output to the screen can be simply redirected to a printer, to the serial port, or to a disk file. Users can define their own streams as well. This is a feature that C language programmers find very useful but with which BASIC programmers are unfamiliar, since streams are not offered in most BASIC language environments.

Multivalued functions in GCLISP provide efficiency by allowing the user to retain multiple data values from a single function. Closures, which are functional objects with state attributes, can support object-oriented programming styles and message passing.

GCLISP will be constantly upgraded. Planned new features are a LISP compiler and a run-time library. While the version of GCLISP used to research this book was designed only for the IBM PC line of machines and compatibles, future releases will run on the Data General/One, the DEC Rainbow, and the Wang PC. A special version of GCLISP is being developed to run in a multitasking, virtual-memory operating system environment on the 80286 series of machines like the IBM PC-AT. Gold Hill Computers will provide an easy upgrade procedure for those owning earlier releases.

I have made many calls to Gold Hill Computers for technical assistance to better understanding their GCLISP package. I have also talked with other users of this package. In all cases, Gold Hill Computers has received rave reviews for their customer support facilities. If someone is not immediately available to answer a question, you can expect a return phone call within a very short time. The company backs their product and supports those who purchase it. You cannot ask for more than this.

The scarcity of experienced LISP programmers and the expense of LISP machines have hindered rapid progress in applying artificial intelligence. GCLISP helps to overcome both of these obstacles. It is a very powerful LISP development package designed with teaching in mind. GCLISP can effectively train an individual or a whole software team to program in LISP on inexpensive personal computers.

GCLISP is packaged with a new edition of *LISP*, a book written by Patrick H. Winston and Berthold K. P. Horn (Professor Winston is director of the Artificial Intelligence Laboratory at MIT.) *LISP* was updated in 1984 to the industry-supported Common LISP standard. The *Common LISP Reference Manual,* written by Guy L. Steele Jr. is also included with the GCLISP package. This manual should provide definitive answers to most questions programmers may have about Common LISP. Both of these books will aid the person who wants to learn to program in Common LISP, but they are especially useful after a firm basis in LISP has been gained.

The San Marco LISP Explorer

To initiate and train the beginner, the GCLISP package is equipped with the San Marco LISP Explorer. This is a beautiful on-screen tutorial that is as versatile as it is thorough. Developed by Patrick Winston and San Marco Associates, the tutorial is arranged logically and with some thought to the psychology of teaching.

The San Marco LISP Explorer is an interactive tutorial that guides the student through LISP programming techniques such as searching, pattern matching, rule-based experts, and natural language recognition. Each lesson includes a practice period (if desired), or you can practice any time you want by entering the GCLISP interpreter with the press of a single key. Pressing another key will put you back in the tutorial.

Teaching is done with a combination of text, examples, and slide shows. The latter incorporates simple on-screen graphics that are sometimes animated or manipulated to stress a point or to make a presentation that is more clearly understood through pictures than through words. Incidentally, all graphics are formed from the standard IBM PC text character set, so the slide show can be used with either the monochrome or color graphics modes on the IBM PC.

As a further learning aid, the GCLIP interpreter environment allows access to the On-Line Help facility that documents every GCLISP function, variable, and type. This is an excellent aid when a quick reference is needed by a programmer who has reached an area that requires the use of unfamiliar functions, or when the use of a certain feature is a bit muddy in the mind.

The GMACS Full-Screen Editor

An essential tool for any serious software development system is a good full-screen editor. In GCLISP this editor is called GMACS. It is an intelligent, EMACS-like editor. GMACS aids the programmer by performing such tasks as parentheses matching, automatic code indentation, and evaluation of LISP expressions within the edit buffer. Other GCLISP development tools allow the programmer to trace procedure calls, pretty-print code, backtrace the execution stack, and execute programs one step at a time.

GMACS is entered in one of two ways: by typing the Ctrl + E sequence or by entering

(ed filename)

while under the GCLISP interpreter. A standard Ctrl + C allows editor exit. (note: Ctrl + X does the same thing.)

GMACS is more comprehensive and more difficult to learn than a line editor such as EDLIN in MS-DOS, but the documentation is very good so it shouldn't take too many hours to become comfortable with GMACS, even if you've never used a full-screen editor before.

GCLISP Debugging Utilities

GCLISP offers several debugging routines that are thorough and easily accessed and understood. The GCLISP debugging utilities include:

1. Break or Ctrl + Break
2. Backtrace or Ctrl + B
3. Trace
4. Step
5. PPRINT

Break is a function that suspends the current listener, which in LISP is the part of the interpreter that reads your program after it has been loaded into RAM. There are 36 different listeners. When the current listener is suspended, you go to a new listener, but you still have all of the system services available. In other words, your program is still resident and can be restarted at the break point by typing

(continue)

Backtrace displays LISP forms that have not completed evaluation and can be used at any time. However, it is most helpful at a break or error level. When there is more than one incomplete form, as would be the case with a break or error detection, Backtrace displays the most recently encountered form first. The next uncompleted form is displayed second, and so on.

Trace dynamically displays the input values and the output values of functions. Put more simply, Trace displays the arguments and returned values of each function. Trace is very useful when the interface between procedures is not correctly implemented.

Step allows the programmer to view each step in the evaluation of a LISP form and to control the progress of these evaluations. Step is input along with a form. It then prints the form to the screen before evaluation occurs. The programmer can then select from a series of options whether to step to the next level in the form, return the value of the form, step to the next level up, enter break level, etc. If you are a bit confused and don't know which option you want, simply type a question mark (?) and the option list appears on the monitor screen along with each option's command sequence.

The acronym *PPRINT* for "pretty print" displays text in an easily read format. It allows the programmer to analyze the components of a LISP function more easily. Basically, PPRINT reformats a procedure for display in what might be termed standard LISP style. It spreads long evaluations over several lines to break down the evaluation into short, easy-to-read constructs.

PROGRAMMING IN LISP

Learning to write simple programs in LISP is a fairly easy procedure, especially for those who have some experience with other high-level languages such as BASIC. The syntax will seem quite weird at first, but after a few weeks of practice, you will begin to think in LISP. Most books about LISP teach LISP in a vacuum and do not refer to other languages. This method has its merits; it precludes the reinforcement of bad habits such as thinking of everything in terms of mathematics. Mathematical thinking is more appropriate to computer languages such as BASIC, FORTRAN, and C.

But the plain truth is that most microcomputer programmers who take up LISP initially learned to program in BASIC, thus, they automatically think of LISP programming in terms of BASIC programs. A typical scenario: "I know how to write a FOR-NEXT loop in BASIC and I know how it can be used to good advantage. Now, how do I do the same thing in LISP?"

Some teachers abhor this kind of analogical thinking, but it is my feeling that BASIC programmers fare better when the new language they are learning is taught with references and comparisons to the language they already know quite well. LISP can do anything BASIC can do, and BASIC can do anything that LISP can do, but it is easier to program certain applications in LISP than it is to program the same applications in BASIC. Conversely, it is also easier to program certain applications in BASIC than it is in LISP. These same analogies apply to most other languages.

This book teaches the fundamentals of LISP by mating reference to equivalent or similar BASIC programs. After the student has learned the fundamentals of LISP, he/she can move deeper into the language and begin to grasp the real purpose for which LISP was developed.

Unfortunately, many people purchase a LISP programming package thinking that the language will quickly transport them into the world of artificial intelligence. They believe that any program written in LISP is an exercise in artificial intelligence. This is simply and utterly untrue. Artificial intelligence applications can be written in any language—once you understand what the AI is all about. LISP only makes writing such applications easier than most other languages.

For example, let's assume that you know BASIC inside and out. You are familiar with all the statements and functions in BASIC and feel quite comfortable programming in a BASIC environment. Assignment: Write a BASIC program that calculates the exact positions of the planets of this solar system for the next 400 years. You must do this by using only your knowledge of BASIC programming. You cannot resort to manuals on astronomy that will provide you with angular vectors on planetary orbits, orbit periods, and interrelationships. Ready. Set. Go!

Unless you are an astronomer or astrophysicist, this assignment will be impossible to complete. The notion of writing such a program, based only your knowledge of BASIC programming, is a ridiculous one. And it's just as ridiculous to assume that by learning LISP, you can automatically write programs in the area of artificial intelligence.

BASIC offers the tools necessary to write the planetary orbit program, just as LISP offers the tools to write artificial intelligence programs. In both cases, all that is missing is knowledge of the particular field. In the latter example, the principles behind artificial intelligence must be learned before any serious attempts can be made at programming. Once this knowledge is gained, LISP offers the tools necessary to convert it into working applications.

To put this another way: Knowing how to saw a board, hammer a nail, and paint a wall doesn't mean necessarily qualify you to build a house. This book discusses the basics of hammering a nail in LISP, sawing a board through LISP procedures, and painting a wall using LISP forms, but it will take far more study before you actually build an artificial intelligence program.

LISP is still a relatively new language, especially where microcomputers are concerned. "Practical" artificial intelligence still does not exist. But AI is the object of much research and development. As artificial intelligence becomes better defined, the programmer who knows LISP and development tools it offers will be in the best position to take advantage of this new technology and go more deeply into its now mystical environment.

Chapter 2

Beginning LISP

Learning to program in LISP is no more difficult than learning to program in most other languages. This book assumes that you are already familiar with microcomputers and that you have some knowledge of BASIC. BASIC is used almost universally by beginning microcomputer users, it is quite versatile, and it is easy to learn. If BASIC is the only computer language you know, you will have to discard some of the prejudices that come from using it. One major shortcoming of BASIC, other than its unstructured design, is that it tends to hide from the programmer the machine operations each statement or function call invokes. Therefore, moving from BASIC to other languages can sometimes be more difficult than moving from Pascal or C into a LISP environment. However, knowledge of BASIC is certainly an aid to learning LISP when compared with teaching LISP to someone who knows no computer language.

Unlike most mathematically based computer languages, LISP deals more with *lists* of items. In LISP, a list is composed of *elements*. These elements may be other lists that in turn, contain their own elements. Each element in a list can be broken down into *atoms*, which are list elements that cannot be broken down further.

SIMPLE LISTS

LISP quickly accustoms one to parentheses ( ). Parentheses are used to contain list elements. In LISP, you will always see an open parenthesis "(" and a close parenthesis ")" on every program line. For example:

```
(COW PIG HORSE)
```

In LISP, this is a list. Not a list of words, not a list of letters, not a list of letters and spaces but, simply, a list. For now, what the list contains is unimportant. This is a single list, which is clear immediately from the single set of parentheses. The open parenthesis signals the start of a list, the close parenthesis signals the end.

Elements and Atoms

Within the parentheses that form the list are the list elements. In this example, the list contains three elements: COW, PIG, and HORSE. These elements are also atoms, because they cannot be broken down further. Now, BASIC programmers will say that these elements can be reduced to the letters in each word. While this is true in BASIC, it does not apply to this discussion of LISP. List elements are separated by a space. Therefore the first list element, COW, is separate from the rest. The word COW is an atom. It is an entity unto itself. LISP sees this word as a separate, unique entity and *not* as a series of the letters C, O, and W.

We now know that the other two list elements in this example are also atoms, since they cannot be broken down in smaller elements. This example can thus be described as a single list containing three elements, each of which is an atom.

Let's look at a slightly different example:

```
((COW) (PIG) (HORSE))
```

This is another list. How does it differ from the previous example? For a start, there are four sets of parentheses instead of only one set. We stated earlier that a list is begun by an open parenthesis and ended by a close parenthesis. Since this example shows four sets of parentheses (open/close), you could say that this example shows four different lists—and this is a correct assumption!

Let's dissect this example. The first open parenthesis begins a list with three elements. This was the case with the first example. In this example, however, the first list contains three other lists, each of which is an element of the first list. Each of the inner lists contain only a single element, and each of these elements is an atom. The first list contains these three lists:

```
(COW)
(PIG)
(HORSE)
```

It is sometimes difficult to grasp the fact that, in LISP, a list may contain many items, only one item (as in the above example), or no items at all. At present, it is not necessary to know why a list may be referenced that contains no items, only that it can and does happen.

Remember, an atom is an element that has been broken down into its smallest parts or units. In LISP, all numbers, individual letters, and symbols are atoms; whole words are also atoms. Whether an item is an atom or an element depends on how the various quantities are written in a LISP program. The following example demonstrates this:

```
(C O W)
```

What is this? We know it is a single list because of the single set of parentheses. But how many elements does this list contain? The answer is three because the list contains three individual letters, each of which is an atom. The following example shows another list:

```
(COW)
```

This list contains only one element that is also an atom. It cannot be broken down into individual letters because of the way it is written into the list.

Embedded Lists

Consider the following list:

```
(COW (C O W) PIG)
```

This is another example of a list that contains several elements, including an internal list. The outer list contains three elements. They are:

```
COW
(C O W)
PIG
```

The first element, COW, is an atom, and so is PIG, the last element. But the second element is not an atom: It is an internal or embedded list that contains three elements of its own, each of which is an atom.

The following example is a bit more complex:

```
(COW (COW PIG HORSE) (PIG HORSE) HORSE)
```

Here the outer list contains 4 items:

```
COW
(COW PIG HORSE)
(PIG HORSE)
HORSE
```

The two embedded lists contain three and two elements, respectively. Embedded lists contain their own elements, which may be atoms or more embedded lists. Later you will learn about LISP functions that allow the retrieval of specific elements from long, complex lists, but for now it is important to know the difference between a list element and an atom. All lists in LISP can be broken down into elements and these elements can be broken down into atoms (if they are not already atoms). The atom is the smallest quantity that can be retrieved from a list.

Here is another list that looks a bit odd:

```
(() ())
```

This example is a list that contains two embedded lists, each of which contains no elements. The outer list contains two inner lists, which means it has two elements. The inner lists have no elements. This is a *NULL list*. Look at the parentheses to determine the contents of NULL lists. The above example contains three sets of parentheses. The outer parentheses contain two sets of inner parentheses. Note that the first inner list is separated from the second by a space. This marks the end of the first inner list and the start of the second inner list. We will later discover the many uses of NULL lists and learn how elements can be inserted during a program run.

Symbols, Numbers, and Atoms

Throughout the previous discussion, all lists contained list elements composed of either other lists or atoms. In LISP, there are two basic types of atoms: *symbols* and *numbers*. Any atom composed of numbers only is not a symbol; any atom composed of letters, letters and numbers, or any other characters is a symbol. This is the definition we will use in exploring Common LISP, even though the definition is an older one. Today, almost any LISP object (with a few exceptions) is considered to be an atom. This can be confusing, so for now let's think of symbols and numbers as atoms and other LISP objects as nonatoms.

The following list demonstrates the difference between symbols and numbers:

```
((A B C) (1234))
```

14

This list contains two list elements, both of which are also lists. The first embedded list contains three elements, the letters A, B, and C. Each of these letters is an atom and each is also a symbol.

The second embedded list contains one element, the number 1234. This number is an atom, but it is not a symbol because, according to our definition, numbers are not symbols. Here's another example:

```
(AB C123 34)
```

This is a single list that contains three elements. Each of the elements is an atom. The first element is a symbol. The second element is also a symbol because it contains a combination of letters and numbers. The third element is a number.

LISTS OF GREATER COMPLEXITY

Our discussion of lists, elements, atoms, symbols, and numbers has used fairly simple list examples. However, lists can often be very complex, depending on the grouping that is necessary to perform a program function. The following is a more complex list:

```
(ABC (DEF (GHI)))
```

How many lists are shown in this example?

The answer is easily found by counting the parentheses. There are three sets of parentheses, so three lists are represented. The outer list contains two elements. The first is the atom ABC, which is also a symbol. The second element is an embedded list. But this embedded list also contains its own embedded list. The first inner list contains the atom (and symbol) DEF. Its second element is an inner list of the atom (and symbol) GHI. This entire quantity can be described as a list within a list with a list.

The complexity can be further increased with:

```
(ABC (()) (DEF (GHI) ()))
```

Again, count the sets of parentheses to determine the total number of lists this expression contains. There are 6 sets, so there are 6 lists; the outer list contains 5 embedded lists. The outer list contains the atom and symbol ABC along with an inner list containing a NULL inner list; an inner list containing the atom DEF, plus another list containing GHI, plus another list with a NULL value.

Lists in LISP programs can seem quite complex at first glance, but after you learn the simple rules for reading list contents the difficulty vanishes. It is absolutely essential that you know how to read the contents of lists, because LISP programs are composed entirely of lists. Lists contain not only items to be processed but processing commands as well. In LISP, mathematical operations are carried out within lists. Adding the values 5 and 4 requires a list containing the proper values and the mathematical operation symbol. Remember, LISP sees nearly everything as a list broken down into elements and then into atoms that are either symbols or numbers.

Once you get the simple list outline in the previous paragraph firmly fixed in your mind, your journey through LISP will be fairly easy. To read a LISP program, it is necessary to read the contents of list after list.

EXPRESSIONS

In LISP, an *expression* is just what we have been dealing with in previous examples: the collection of atoms and lists, symbolically expressed, usually in a program. Atoms are composed of symbols and/or numbers. A collection of atoms is called a list. A list may be composed of other lists and atoms. The way these quantities are expressed in LISP programs is called an expression. An expression, then, is the collection of atoms, lists, and embedded lists that express a collection of data the programmer wishes to use for processing.

DATA TYPES

Data types in LISP have already been discussed, they are simply the atoms, symbols, numbers, and lists that will be dealt with time and again in a LISP environment. In BASIC, we only have to deal with strings and numbers as data types, although numeric data types are broken down into integer, single precision, and double precision types. The subcategorization of numeric data types also occurs in LISP. This will be discussed in a later chapter. For now, remember that major LISP data types include atoms, numbers, symbols, and lists.

To review, remember that a list is begun by the open parentheses and ended by the close parenthesis. List contents are called elements. A list element may be an atom or another list. If an atom contains only numeric characters, then it is a number; if it contains alphabetic and/or numeric characters or any other character types, it is called a symbol. List elements are separated by spaces. Lists can be broken down into their individual elements, and atoms are the smallest quantity possible in a LISP program; they cannot be broken down into smaller quantities.

If you do not understand the difference between list elements and atoms or between numbers and symbols, or if you don't know how to read a list, then reread this chapter. Study its contents until you know them by heart. Future chapters depend on your knowledge of this chapter in order to take you into the full LISP environment.

Chapter 3

LISP Mathematics

Since computers are mathematical machines, most computer languages are mathematically oriented. For example, in BASIC it is far easier to program highly complex text-processing operations. BASIC allows us to simply type in the formula almost as it would appear in a textbook. The handling of other types of variables or constants is more difficult.

LISP is different. It is designed to make it easy to process collections of data without regard to whether they are numeric or text. LISP allows us to handle diversified items of data in much the same way the human mind processes the same information: as a collection of *possibly related* data.

However, in any language it is necessary to be able to express purely mathematical operations easily and LISP is no exception. BASIC programmers will find that LISP handles mathematics in a slightly odd fashion. Once you grasp the concept, you should be able to express quickly and accurately any mathematical equation in LISP as easily as in BASIC or any other mathematically based computer language.

SIMPLE LISP MATH

The following list will introduce you to LISP math:

```
(+ 4 5)
```

This list contains three list elements. The first element is the plus sign (+). Is this element another list, or is it an atom, a number, or a symbol? By the rules outlined in the previous chapter, you know that the plus sign is both an atom and it is also a symbol. (If it's an atom, then it has to be either a symbol or a number. The plus sign is a symbol because it does not contain a purely numerical character or set of characters.

The remaining two list elements are numbers (as well as atoms) because they only represent numbers and not another type of character. The combination of atoms forms a list. The list, in this example, is an expression. What does it express? It obviously expresses the mathematical operation of adding the number 4 to the number 5.

If you are new to LISP, you are undoubtedly a bit awed by the placement of the mathematical operator. In BASIC the expression would have been written as 4 + 5. In LISP, the mathematical operation is specified *first*. This is called *prefix notation* and, though it is less common than postfix ("Polish") notation, it is not that unusual a computer language.

You will also notice that no equality operator (=) is used, nor is one necessary. The LISP expression returns the value of 4 added to 5. Put simply, this expression equals 9. Here is a more complex addition operation:

```
(+ (+ 4 5) (+ 3 1))
```

This is also a list, but it contains two embedded lists. Each of these lists contains three elements that are atoms. Three different mathematical operations are specified in this LISP expression. When performed, the expression equals 13. In BASIC, this expression would read:

```
(4+5) + (3+1)
```

In the preceding examples, the plus sign (+) was defined as an atom that is a symbol. It is also known as a *procedure*. This is an appropriate name, since the plus sign tells LISP how to process the list in which it is found. The procedure always heads the list.

Besides the plus sign, the other common math symbols are available to the LISP programmer. This example shows subtraction:

```
(- 5 4)
```

This expression evaluates to 1, since 5 − 4 = 1. Remember, because LISP uses prefix notation, the mathematical procedure heads the list and the values to be applied to this procedure follow. Let's combine the two mathematical procedures already discussed:

```
(+ (- 5 2) (+ 14 6))
```

This expression.evaluates to 23 and is equivalent to:

```
(5 - 2) + (14 + 6)
```

What value does the following expression produce?

```
(* 4 3)
```

If you answered 12, you are correct. The procedure specified by the asterisk is multiplication. The following expression uses the division procedure:

```
(\ 8 4)
```

It evaluates to 2.

As you grow accustomed to prefix notation, mathematical operations in LISP will become quite simple. All of the previous examples used only two numbers. The following expression is an expansion of a previous simple example:

```
(\ 16 2 2)
```

This expression evaluates to 4 and is equivalent to:

```
16 / 2 / 2
```

The stated mathematical procedure applies to all values in the list. Here is another example using the multiplication procedure:

```
(* 3 4 5)
```

This is equivalent to:

```
3 * 4 * 5
```

Both equal 60.

MORE COMPLEX MATHEMATICS

When more complex mathematical formulas are used in a LISP program, it is necessary to increase the depth of a list, that is, embed additional lists. Consider the following formula:

```
X = 14/22 * 12
```

This operation requires two procedures, division and multiplication. In LISP, this is expressed as:

```
(* (/ 14 22) (12))
```

Note that the division of 14 by 22 occurs in one embedded list, while in the second embedded list there is no procedure but only the number itself. The second embedded list is unnecessary because it does not contain a procedure. Therefore, this expression could also appear as:

```
(* (/ 14 22) 12)
```

In either expression, the returned value is the same.

Now, examine the following formula:

```
x = ((14+3+5)/(34-28)) / (17*.33)
```

In this example, four different mathematical operations are required: addition, subtraction, multiplication, and division. The equivalent LISP expression is:

```
(/ (/ (+ 14 3 5) (- 34 28)) (* 17 .33))
```

There are five separate lists in this expression (note the five sets of parentheses). The outer list contains two embedded lists, the first of which contains two more embedded lists. Each of the five lists has a mathematical procedure symbol.

Let's go even further with the following formula:

```
x = (14 + 2 - 1) / (3*4+2)
```

This formula also uses four different mathematical operations. The LISP expression looks like this:

```
(/ (+ 14 2 -1) (+ (*3 4) (2)))
```

This could be expressed differently, but this example is the most simple and direct.

Be aware that LISP performs mathematical operations from the inside out; that is, LISP evaluates all expressions from the inside to the outside. For example, the expression

```
(/ (* 4 3) 2)
```

is written as

```
(4 * 3) / 2
```

in standard notation. LISP first evaluates the inner procedure and arrives at the number 12 (4 × 3 = 12). The outer procedure is then evaluated, and the final output is equal to 2. There is nothing unusual about inside-out evaluation; it is the method used by most microcomputer languages.

HIGHER MATH FUNCTIONS

Most LISP implementations offer the higher math functions that microcomputer users have come to expect from using BASIC and other high-level languages. These include the standard trigonometric and geometric functions such as square root, exponent, cosine, sine, etc. For example, the following expression equals 3:

```
(SQRT 9)
```

Obviously, SQRT is the square-root function with the number 9 as its argument. Assuming that you are now more familiar with prefix notation, the following expression you should be able to evaluate the following expression:

```
(/ (SQRT 4) (* 1.5 2.3))
```

In BASIC, this line can be written as:

```
SQR(4)/(1.5*2.3)
```

In LISP, we treat the more complex functions such as SQRT, COS, and EXP just as we do the common mathematical operators (*, +, −, /). No extra parentheses are necessary because even complex math procedures are still procedures and *not* functions as they are in BASIC.

ARRAYS

Both single-dimension and multidimensional arrays are possible in Common LISP, although some implementations such as GCLISP limit the user to single-dimension arrays only. However, it is far easier to explain the construction of arrays using a single-dimension grid rather than using one with two or more grids.

MAKE-ARRAY is the Common LISP primitive (more about primitives in the next chapter) that is used to set up space to store the array elements. To form a single-dimension array to hold four elements, we can use the following procedure:

```
(SETF X (MAKE-ARRAY 4))
```

Now, X represents an array that has been dimensioned to hold four elements. The element positions are numbered 0, 1, 2, and 3 and are accessed by naming these positions. At this point an array has been structured, but it contains no information other than the value 0 (zero) in each of the four positions. This value is assigned through the default operation of MAKE-ARRAY.

To place information in the array, we use the Common LISP function called AREF. This is an acronym for ARRAY REFERENCE, which is used both for placing information in a dimensioned array and for retrieving information from it. This function requires two arguments. The first is the name of the array and the second is the array position:

```
(AREF X 0)
```

This line allows access to the first or zero element position of the array represented by symbol X, which was dimensioned previously by MAKE-ARRAY. When using AREF, make certain that an array has already been dimensioned: otherwise, an error message will be displayed.

SETF, the general assignment primitive in Common LISP, is used in conjunction with AREF to write information to the array. The following example places an object in the first position of array X:

```
(SETF (AREF X 0) 14)
```

AREF is fed the name of the array and its position. SETF assigns this position the number 14. Now the procedure

```
(AREF X 0)
```

will return the atom 14.

The following lines assign the remaining three positions of array X:

24

```
(SETF  (AREF  X  1)  7
       (AREF  X  2)  2
       (AREF  X  3)  28)
```

We now have a fully assigned array with the values:

```
14
7
2
28
```

contained in its four positions.

Mathematical operations can be performed with these values by treating the array positions as objects. For instance:

```
(/  (AREF  X  0)  (AREF  X  1))
```

divides the number in the first array position by the one in the second array position. The breaks down to:

```
(/  14  2)
```

for a value of 7. To add all of the array elements use:

```
(+  (AREF  X  0)  (AREF  X  1)
 (AREF  X  2)  (AREF  X  3))
```

This is the same as:

```
(+  14  2  7  28)
```

Both expressions give the value 51.

LISP is not known as a mathematical language since it is most efficient at handling lists of objects. However, mathematical programming is necessary for many applications and Common LISP is equipped with an excellent set of math primitives to tackle such work. You may still hear complaints from those not versed in LISP about the language's weak math abilities, but this is no longer true. Common LISP offers the standard math capabilities found in most computer languages.

Math functions were introduced early on in this book because most programmers in other languages are familiar with them. This chapter's discussion of them should make it easier for the student to begin to tackle lists of objects.

Chapter 4

LISP Primitives

Any procedure supplied by LISP is called a *primitive*. LISP primitives vary, depending on the LISP software package used for writing and running a program. However, some primitives are common to most or all LISP interpreters and compilers. These are discussed in this chapter.

COMMON PRIMITIVES

In the previous chapter on mathematical operations, we discussed some procedures that can be classified as primitives. For example:

```
(+ 14 12)
```

uses the addition procedure (+). This can also be called a primitive, since it is a procedure provided by the LISP programming environment. But the most important components in a LISP program are lists, which, as we already know, may be comprised of letters, words, numbers, and other lists. LISP uses many primitives designed specifically to process information in lists.

FIRST

Common LISP uses the FIRST primitive to extract the first element from a list. This primitive is better known to more experienced LISP programmers as CAR, but Common LISP calls it by the more appropriate name. The following example demonstrates the use of FIRST:

```
(FIRST '(A B C))
```

Notice the single quote symbol preceding the list (A B C). The single quote is important because it identifies the following expression as a list, rather than another procedure or an assigned variable. In the above example, the expression evaluates to A, which is the first element in the list.

The single quote is somewhat analogous to the double quotes that surround string constants in BASIC. Take the following BASIC program examples:

```
PRINT "A";"B";"C"

PRINT A;B;C
```

In the first example, the quotes indicate that the letters themselves are to be written to the monitor screen. In the second example, the absence of quotes indicates that the *values* of the variables A, B, and C are to be displayed.

The single quote in LISP means much the same thing. Therefore:

```
(FIRST A)
```

commands that the first element in the list represented by the variable A is to be returned.

Let's try some more examples of the primitive FIRST:

```
(FIRST '(HELLO GOODBYE SO LONG))
```

This expression evaluates to HELLO since it is the first element in the list. Does the following expression evaluate to HELLO?

```
(FIRST '((HELLO) GOODBYE SO LONG))
```

The answer is no! The first element in the outer list is not the atom HELLO, but another list that contains the atom HELLO. This example therefore evaluates to (HELLO) rather than to HELLO.

Here is a similar example:

28

```
(FIRST '((HELLO GOODBYE FAR)
         GOODBYE SO LONG))
```

This expression evaluates to the list:

```
(HELLO GOODBYE FAR)
```

since it is the first element of the outer list.

The following expression contains a NULL list (a list with no elements) as the first embedded element of the outer list:

```
(FIRST '(() GOODBYE FAR))
```

This expression evaluates to NIL, which is LISP's way of telling you that the first element of the outer list is an embedded list that contains no elements.

Numbers are atoms and are treated just like any other list element. The following expression contains both numbers and alphabetic characters:

```
(FIRST '(1234 HELLO FAR432))
```

The expression evaluates to 1234, which is the first element in the outer list.

REST

Now that we have explored FIRST, the LISP primitive that returns the first element in a list, let's look at another that is appropriately named REST. This primitive is known in other versions of LISP as CDR (pronounced "coulder"); it returns all but the first element in a list. For example:

```
(REST '(HELLO GOODBYE FAR))
```

evaluates to GOODBYE FAR because these are the last two elements of the list.

What does the following expression evaluate to?

```
(REST '(HELLO (GOODBYE FAR)))
```

The answer is (GOODBYE FAR), an embedded list that forms the second and last elements of the indicated list. Note that this example evaluates to another list, not to the atoms GOODBYE and HELLO. If the returned value is a NULL list, then LISP returns NIL.

Here is another example of NIL:

```
(REST ' (HELLO))
```

REST returns all but the first element of the list. Since there is only one element, there is no list element to return. LISP returns NIL to let you know that the expression evaluates to nothing.

Now let's use our knowledge of the primitives FIRST and LAST to write an expression that will evaluate to the second element of the list:

```
(HELLO GOODBYE FAR)
```

We know that FIRST returns the first list element and that REST returns all but the first list element. To write an expression that evaluates to the second list element, we combine FIRST and LAST for the following expression:

```
(FIRST (REST ' (HELLO GOODBYE FAR)))
```

This expression says, "Take the FIRST element of the REST of the indicated list." Or, "Take the REST of the indicated list, then take the FIRST of what is left."

LISP evaluates this expression as follows:

1. (REST ' (HELLO GOODBYE FAR))
   Result = GOODBYE FAR

2. FIRST ' (GOODBYE FAR))
   Result = GOODBYE

The expression thus evaluates to the second element in the indicated list. Most versions of LISP contain another primitive called SECOND that returns the second element of a list, so these steps are not necessary. However, the SECOND primitive is built using the primitives FIRST and LAST (to be discussed in a moment) as in the above example. (You will later learn how to build highly complex procedures using the few simple primitives contained in LISP.)

What does the following expression evaluate to?

```
(FIRST (REST ' (HELLO (GOODBYE FAR) FAR)))
```

The answer is the embedded list (GOODBYE FAR), because this is the second element of the indicated list. Notice that in the last two examples the single quote does not follow the first primitive. This tells the primitive FIRST to evaluate the *expression* that follows, not a list. The single quote does follow REST, since this primitive must evaluate a list and not an expression. Remember that the single quote tells LISP to evaluate the literal elements themselves and not the expression.

The following example uses FIRST twice:

```
(FIRST
(FIRST '((A B C) HELLO GOODBYE FAR)))
```

The expression evaluates to A using these steps:

1. FIRST ' ((A B C) HELLO GOODBYE FAR)
   Result = (A B C)   ;Note:This is a list

2. FIRST ' (A B C)
   Result = A

The inner expression is evaluated first since LISP evaluates from inside out. The result is then evaluated. This expression first extracts the first element from the embedded list (A B C). Then FIRST extracts the first element from (A B C), which is A. Remember, FIRST needs a list as its *argument*, i.e., the information on which it is to act. If an atom is returned, an error message will result.

This expression uses REST two times:

```
(REST (REST '(HELLO GOODBYE FAR)))
```

The expression evaluates to FAR, the third (and coincidentally last) element of the specified list. Using REST twice does not return the last element of a list or even the third element but the third element and all the elements that follow it. For example, the following expression evaluates to FAR FARTHER, which are all the elements in the list from the third element onward:

```
(REST
(REST '(HELLO GOODBYE FAR FARTHER)))
```

Literally stated, this expression says, "Take the REST of the REST of the specified list." It follows these steps:

1. REST ' (HELLO GOODBYE FAR FARTHER)
   Result = GOODBYE FAR FARTHER

2. REST ' (GOODBYE FAR FARTHER)
   Result = FAR FARTHER

LAST

Another LISP primitive found in Common LISP is LAST. Taken in conjunction with the previous primitives, you might suspect that LAST returns the last element of a list, but that is

not its function. LAST works a bit differently than FIRST and
REST by returning the last element of a list *as a list*. Technically,
LAST returns the last CONS of a list. (CONS is discussed later
in this chapter.) For now, think of LAST as returning the last list
element as a list rather than as an element. For example:

```
(LAST ' (HELLO GOODBYE FAR))
```

This evaluates to (FAR), which is the last element in the specified
list. Notice that this return is surrounded by parentheses, indicating
that this element is a list containing a single element. The returned
list in this example contains a single element that is an atom, the
following example returns a list within a list:

```
(LAST ' (HELLO GOODBYE (FAR NEAR)))
```

This expression evaluates to ((FAR NEAR)), which is the list that
is the last element of the outer list (HELLO GOODBYE (FAR
NEAR)). The expression

```
(LAST ' (HELLO))
```

evaluates to (HELLO), which is the first, last, and only element
in the specified list. The following expression evaluates to NIL:

```
(LAST ' (HELLO GOODBYE FAR ()))
```

LISP returns NIL because the last element in the specified list is
an embedded list with no elements.

We can combine the three LISP primitives in the following expression:

```
(FIRST
(REST
(LAST ' (HELLO GOODBYE (FAR NEAR AWAY))))))
```

This expression might seem to evaluate to NEAR using the following procedure:

1. LAST ' (HELLO GOODBYE (FAR NEAR AWAY))
   Return = (FAR NEAR AWAY)

2. REST ' (FAR NEAR AWAY)
   Return = NEAR AWAY

3. FIRST ' (NEAR AWAY)
   Return = NEAR

However, this is definitely not the case! Again, watch out for LAST, because it doesn't work like FIRST and REST. In fact, the result of:

```
(LAST '(HELLO GOODBYE (FAR NEAR AWAY)))
```

is not:

```
(FAR NEAR AWAY)
```

but the embedded list:

```
((FAR NEAR AWAY))
```

Therefore:

```
(REST '((FAR NEAR AWAY)))
```

evaluates to NIL. This happens because the embedded list is the first element of the object list. After the first element is removed, nothing remains and the return is NIL. Finally:

```
(FIRST '())
```

is still NIL. In this example NIL is represented by a NULL list or ( ).

FIRST, REST, LAST, and other LISP primitives such as SECOND, THIRD, FOURTH, etc., can be used to extract data in a complex fashion from very complex lists. You can use these primitives with others to build lists that are comprised of elements from still other lists. It is important to understand how they work and what they return given certain types of list arguments.

SETF

So far the examples in this book have used either constants or the actual atoms or list elements to be evaluated. However, it is quite easy to assign variables to these values. Unlike other languages, LISP does not use the equality operator (=) to make assignments. A LISP primitive is used instead. In Common LISP, SETF is the primitive used to assign values to variables (usually called *symbols* in LISP). For example:

```
(SETF X '14)
```

assigns the value 14 to the variable X. X will now evaluate to 14 until a reassignment is made. We can use the variable X in an expression such as:

```
(/ X 7)
```

What does this expression evaluate to? If you said 2, you are absolutely WRONG! It evaluates to a type-mismatch error (assuming that SETF was used to assign variable X a value of '14). Why? Remember our brief discussion on the use of the single quote, which tells LISP to evaluate the constant as though it were a BASIC expression enclosed in quotation marks. The expression:

```
(SETF X '14)
```

is the LISP equivalent of the BASIC program line:

```
X$ = "14"
```

LISP makes no differentiation between character and numeric variables, at least in the symbols used to represent them.

SETF assigns a numeric value to a variable in the following manner:

```
(SETF X 14)
```

Notice that the single quote has been dropped completely. The *value* 14 evaluates to the number 14. Therefore X will evaluate to the number 14, as opposed to the characters 1 and 4. Now we can write an expression using X as the symbol for the *number* 14 as in:

```
(/ X 7)
```

This expression evaluates to the number 2.

Here is an example of how SETF assigns a list to a variable:

```
(SETF L '(HELLO GOODBYE FAR))
```

The symbol L will now evaluate to the list (HELLO GOODBYE FAR). For example:

```
(FIRST L)
```

This expression evaluates to HELLO, the first element of the list assigned to symbol L. The symbol L can also be used to represent its assigned list when used with other LISP primitives.

SETF and certain other Common LISP procedures are not classified as primitives but as *special forms*; they generally are control procedures. The evaluation of special forms usually produces a value.

Several other Common LISP primitives are used to make symbol assignments. One that you will probably see quite often is SETQ. This primitive is common to most other dialects of LISP and was probably retained by Common LISP to maintain tradition. For all intents and purposes, SETF replaces SETQ, and the two can be used interchangeably. Use SETF to make assignments, because it will eventually replace SETQ and others like SET and RPLACA. SETF does what these do in a single, easy-to-remember special form.

SETF can make single assignments to symbols, as in:

```
(SETF X 44)
```

but it can also assign groups of symbols. The following demonstrates the assignment of four different symbols to four different values:

```
(SETF A 1
      B 14
      C '(X Y Z)
      D 'HELLO)
```

This could have been written as:

```
(SETF A 1 B 14 C '(X Y Z) D 'HELLO)
```

but the former presentation is much easier to understand. Writing LISP procedures that are readily understood is an important part of programming in LISP—or any other language. LISP doesn't care where you start a new line or whether you start one at all. It does care about the proper placement of those parentheses and spaces in relation to the primitives and objects used to write a program.

Observe other LISP programs to gain an idea of the accepted presentations or forms by which LISP procedures are written. These formats have nothing to do with the actual execution of the program but they do affect the readability of the source code. By using generally accepted formats, you can be assured that others will understand your LISP applications easily. More importantly, programming in proper LISP format offers less chance for confusion and programming errors that can affect the program run.

Use SETF to make more complex assignments by including other LISP primitives. More appropriately, use SETF to change the value of a preassigned symbol. For example:

```
(SETF X '(A B C))
```

```
(SETF (FIRST X) 'T)
```

The first line sets X to represent the list:

```
(A B C)
```

The second line uses SETF to alter the contents of the list represented by X. The FIRST of the original list is A, but the second line resets the FIRST of X to the letter T. You must be careful in making such assignments: You have to know what kind of object FIRST or any other primitive will return from its argument. FIRST returns a list element; replacing it with 'T simply substitutes one list element for another.

The following example is a bit different:

```
(SETF X '(A B C))

(SETF (REST X) 'T)
```

The result of these operations is the list:

```
(A . T)
```

This is a dotted list. If the intention was to produce:

```
(A T)
```

then the programming sequence was in error. REST returns the list that served as its argument as a list minus the first element. To avoid the dotted list, supply SETF with an argument for the replacement of (REST X) that is also a list. The following sequence gives us what we want:

```
(SETF X '(A B C))

(SETF (REST X) '(T))
```

The new value of X is:

```
(A T)
```

A major function of SETF is making replacements such as these in addition to making initial assignments to symbols. In this mode, SETF is similar to using MID$ in BASIC as a *statement*, not as a function in BASIC. For example:

```
10 A$="COMPUTER"
20 MID$(A$,1,3) = "XYZ"
30 PRINT A$
```

Running this program gives the printed output:

```
XYZPUTER
```

SETF is able to make reassignments based upon the retrieved elements of established lists. The retrieval type will depend upon the LISP primitive used to return the desired portion of the list or lists.

LENGTH

The LENGTH primitive is used to determine the number of elements in a list. Don't confuse this primitive with the LEN function common to most dialects of BASIC. LENGTH does not count the number of characters in a string; it is used to count the number of elements in a list. For example:

```
(LENGTH ' (A B C))
```

evaluates to three (3), the number of elements in the specified list.

That was easy, but consider this example:

```
(LENGTH ' (HELLO (A B C) GOODBYE))
```

The specified list contains two atoms, HELLO and GOODBYE, plus an embedded list that contains three elements. This expression still evaluates to three, since there are three elements in the *specified* list. The embedded list, regardless of its contents, is considered only a single element of the outer list. The LENGTH primitive gives the contents of a list on an element basis. This is useful when lists are built from other lists or from data typed in from the computer keyboard.

BUILDING YOUR OWN PROCEDURES

It bears repeating here that, in LISP, a *primitive* is a procedure or function that is a built-in part of the LISP interpreter or compiler language set. In many cases these may be thought of as functions that are constructed from combinations of other primitives. A *procedure* specifies how something is to be computed, and a *program* is a sequence of procedures designed to accomplish a task. These three definitions are a bit muddy and, frankly, it is sometimes arguable as to just what constitutes a procedure, a function, a program, or even a primitive in LISP.

While LISP programming packages come with a large number of primitives, the programmer will usually find it necessary to build more to suit particular programming applications. A new procedure built from an existing one is usually known as a *function*, although all LISP primitives are often called functions. It is more important to know what these tools do, however, than to know exactly what they are called. *Procedure abstraction* is a common phrase in LISP;

it describes the programmer defining new procedures by combining existing ones.

DEFUN

We can use the DEFUN primitive to build a new procedure in LISP. DEFUN, which is an acronym for Define Function, is used with the following format:

```
(DEFUN <Name of Procedure> (Arguments)
  (Procedure Instructions))
```

As an exercise in the use of DEFUN, let's define a procedure that will return the second item from a list. Most versions of LISP already provide such a primitive, usually named SECOND. Golden Common LISP contains SECOND as well as THIRD. Larger LISP programming packages may contain many more primitives that will return various portions of a list. For this exercise assume that your interpreter does not contain the SECOND primitive. Also assume that you need such a procedure for some programming application.

We learned earlier that combining FIRST and REST creates an expression that returns the second element of a list. This expression is:

```
(FIRST (REST '( <list> )))
```

Remember, REST returns all but the first element in the list. This effectively leaves what was originally the second list element at the head of the list. FIRST then extracts this newly repositioned element.

We use this same sequence with DEFUN to build the SECOND procedure:

```
(DEFUN SECOND (ARGS)
  (FIRST (REST ARGS)))
```

In this example, ARGS is a variable used to contain the list argument. Notice that we use the FIRST/REST procedure to extract the second element from the list named by ARGS. Once defined in a LISP program, the SECOND procedure remains in effect for the duration of that program run. As a result:

```
(SECOND '(HELLO GOODBYE FAR))
```

evaluates to GOODBYE, the second element in the list.

DEFUN makes it quite simple to define many different types of functions. Mathematical formulas are easily inserted (in prefix notation, of course) to build highly complex math functions with little effort. For example, the formula

```
A = PI * R^2.
```

defines the area of a circle. Written as a LISP procedure, it might appear as:

```
(DEFUN CIRAREA (RADIUS)
   (* 3.14159 (* RADIUS RADIUS)))
```

The name of the function is CIRAREA. It accepts a single argument named RADIUS. The procedure body consists of the formula mentioned above but it is in prefix-notation style. The CIRAREA procedure can be used as follows:

```
(CIRAREA 40)
```

This expression evaluates to 5026.54, the area of a circle with a radius of 40.

BASIC programmers will especially appreciate how easily all types of procedures (i.e., functions) can be built in a LISP environment. While it is true that the DEF function can be used in Microsoft BASIC to build some functions, its use is very limited. In LISP, a procedure is simply a subroutine or miniprogram in need of an argument value or values.

As a further example of defining one's own LISP functions, let's return to a little problem discussed earlier in this chapter. You will remember that LAST did not act exactly like FIRST and REST. The latter two primitives extract list elements; LAST extracts the last CONS of a list or returns the last element as an embedded list.

NTH

There is another function similar to LAST, that returns any element named in a list. This is the NTH primitive, so named because it returns the Nth element of a list. In LISP, NTH represents a number that is the argument for the list element that is to be returned. Warning: NTH starts counting at zero instead of one. If you want the third element of a list returned, the numeric or positional argument must be the element position minus 1. This, of course, assumes that you conventionally count the number of list elements in your head, starting with the number 1. Here is an example:

```
(NTH 2 '(A B C D))
```

NTH returns the third element of the list—the letter C. NTH counts the list elements as:

```
 0  1  2  3
(A  B  C  D)
```

Now we have a standard LISP primitive that allows us to pick the list element to be returned. Previously we discussed the LENGTH primitive. You will remember that LENGTH returns the number of elements in a list. It counts elements as we do, starting with the number one, whereas the NTH primitive starts with zero.

We can use DEFUN along with NTH and LENGTH to build a LISP function called LAST-EL that will, indeed, return the last element of a list, just as FIRST returns the first element. The user-defined function follows:

```
(DEFUN LAST-EL (ARG)
   (NTH (- (LENGTH ARG) 1) ARG))
```

This newly defined function returns the last element of a list as an element and not as an embedded list, which is the case with the standard Common LISP primitive LAST. The following procedure extracts the last element from a list:

```
(LAST-EL '(A B C D E F G))
```

This returns the element G, the last element of the list. If LAST were used with this same list, the return would be the list (G).

Building Common LISP functions is not only instructive—it can also lead to hours of fun. A later chapter of this book is devoted exclusively to function building.

BUILDING LISTS

When programming in LISP, it is often necessary to build lists from nonlist objects, from two or more lists, or from a list and a nonlist object. Several primitives deal with this quite efficiently. Many of them seem to operate identically until they are more fully explored. This section will discuss CONS, APPEND, and LIST, three primitives used specifically for list building.

CONS

The CONS primitive in Common LISP accepts two arguments and forms a list. CONS does not necessarily build a single list composed of the two arguments. The actual result depends on the types of arguments CONS is handed.

In addition to being a primitive or LISP function, CONS can also be a data type, which is technically a subtype of list. CONS objects are identified by having two alterable components. These are called FIRST and REST in Common LISP but are more traditionally known as CAR and CDR. The result of a CONS function operation is a CONS list.

The following example uses CONS to produce a single list:

```
(CONS 'A '(B C D))
```

The result of this operation is the list:

```
(A B C D)
```

You can see that CONS has added a new list element, which is its first argument, the letter A, to the front of the second argument, which is a list composed of the elements B, C, and D.

While a single list resulted from this example, it is not always the case. Let's reverse the example and see what happens:

```
(CONS '(B C D) 'A)
```

It would seem that we are now attempting to add the letter A to the back of the list (B C D) for the result of (B C D A). But this will not be the actual result. It instead produces something completely different:

```
((B C D) . A)
```

The period or decimal point separating the two elements of this list make this a *dotted list*. The first argument to CONS becomes the FIRST of the list and the last argument becomes the REST. In the first example, adding a new list element that was a single character to the front of the second list argument formed a new list.

This is the only way the FIRST of the new list and the REST would abide by the CONS definition. Thus:

```
(FIRST '(A B C D))   = A

(REST '(A B C D))   = (B C D)
```

Notice that the FIRST of the list is the *character* A and that the REST of the list is the *list* (B C D). This exactly matches the original CONS arguments.

In the second example we can make the same conclusion:

41

```
(FIRST '((B C D) . A))      = (B C D)

(REST '((B C D) . A))       = A
```

Dotted Lists and Pairs

In the dotted list, the dot is simply for reference and is not thought of as a retrievable element of the list. It is a separator and not a list element.

The second example confirms the CONS rule. The FIRST of this example was the first argument to CONS while the REST of the list was the second example. The dotted list occurs because of the way LISP stores lists in memory. Technically, a list is terminated by NIL, even though that is not apparent from looking at a screen representation of a NIL list. Since the last item in the above example was not a list, a dotted list indicates a list that was terminated by some non-NIL atom. If we use CONS to connect two nonlist objects as in:

```
(CONS 'A 'B)
```

we end up with a *dotted pair*:

```
(A . B)
```

Technically this is not a list but a pair of nonlist objects bound together. Dotted pairs and dotted lists can sometimes be used to advantage, but for the most part they are confusing and a potential source of trouble. Most programmers avoid them.

CONS arguments can be lists, characters, lists and characters, or any combination of embedded lists with embedded characters and so forth on to infinity. The following example uses two list arguments for CONS:

```
(CONS '(A B C) '(D E F))
```

If you think this results in the list:

```
(A B C D E F)
```

then you have forgotten the definition of CONS. For example:

```
(FIRST '(A B C D E F))      = A

(REST '(A B C D E F))       = (B C D E F)
```

This certainly does not reflect the arguments to CONS. The actual list that results from the last CONS example is:

```
((A  B  C)  (D  E  F))
```

Now we can apply the CONS rule:

```
(FIRST '((A  B  C)  (D  E  F))   =  (A  B  C)

(REST '((A  B  C)  (D  E  F))   =  (D  E  F)
```

You can see that the FIRST of the list is the same as the first argument to CONS and the REST of this same list represents the second or last argument to CONS.

CONS can comfortably accept complex lists as arguments:

```
(CONS '(A  B  C  (D  E  F))
      '((G  H  I)  J  K  L))
```

This results in the list:

```
((A  B  C  (D  E  F))  ((G  H  I)  J  K  L))
```

The FIRST and REST of this list will correspond to the first and second arguments to CONS.

APPEND

APPEND is another Common LISP primitive used to construct lists. APPEND works in a manner partly similar to CONS, but there are distinct differences. CONS accepts two arguments and forms a list wherein the FIRST of that list is the first argument and the REST of the list is the second or last argument. APPEND does what its name implies: it concatenates (links) lists into a single list. The following example demonstrates one aspect of APPEND:

```
(APPEND '(A  B  C)  '(D  E  F))
```

The result of this operation is the list:

```
(A  B  C  D  E  F)
```

The second list argument has been *appended* to the first list argument.

APPEND is not limited only to two arguments. For example:

```
(APPEND '(A  B  C)  '(D  E  F)  '(G  H  I))
```

This makes the combined or appended list:

```
(A  B  C  D  E  F  G  H  I)
```

Notice that the FIRST of the appended list is always the first list element which is not the first argument to append.

Remember that all APPEND arguments must be lists. The only exception to this is the last argument, which can be any type of object. If the last argument is not a list, then a dotted list will result. For example, the result from the following operation:

```
(APPEND  '(A  B  C)  'D)
```

is the list:

```
(A  B  C  .  D)
```

Remember, only the last argument to APPEND can be a nonlist object. If you try:

```
(APPEND  'A  '(B  C  D))
```

the following list is returned:

```
(B  C  D)
```

This occurs because the first argument to APPEND is not a list. No error message is generated by GCLISP when it evaluates the above example, although some other Common LISP packages may indicate an error.

The list arguments handed to APPEND can be as complex as you desire. The following demonstrates the linking of complex lists:

```
(APPEND  '((A  B  C)  D  E  F)
         '(G  H  I  (J  K  L)))
```

Here two lists serve as the arguments to APPEND. Each of the two list arguments contains an embedded list. The returned value is the list:

```
((A  B  C)  D  E  F  G  H  I  (J  K  L))
```

This is a single list containing two embedded lists; it is equivalent to linking the first argument to APPEND with the second argument and removing the parentheses that separate the two complex lists.

The FIRST of this list is:

```
(A  B  C)
```

Note that this is a list and also the first element of the complex list. The REST of this list is another list that also contains an embedded list:

```
(D E F G H I (J K L))
```

LIST

LIST, the next list-building primitive in Common LISP, is appropriately named, because it actually creates a list from the objects that serve as its arguments. Like APPEND, it can accept any number of arguments. Unlike APPEND, these arguments can be any type of object.

LIST is used to excellent advantage in many, many programming situations, especially in conjunction with other primitives like APPEND, which requires list arguments. LIST can be used to convert nonlist objects into lists. The following demonstrates one use of LIST:

```
(LIST 'A 'B 'C)
```

Using LIST with single character arguments is the same as saying: "Make a list composed of the letters A, B, and C." The resulting list is:

```
(A B C)
```

We can also use a list as a single argument to LIST. In such cases LIST makes a list out of the argument list:

```
(LIST '(A B C))
```

The result from this is not (A B C) but a list that contains the list argument. In other words, the list argument in this example becomes an embedded list:

```
((A B C))
```

An argument to LIST that is a list itself is thus made a part of another list. The argument is embedded in a new list regardless of whether it is a nonlist or list object. What does the following LIST function return?

```
(LIST 'A '(B C D))
```

If you answered:

```
(A B C D)
```

you are absolutely wrong. The correct answer is:

    (A (B C D))

The letter A becomes an element in the outer list created by LIST to hold its arguments. The second argument also becomes an element in the outer list. But this argument is itself a list, so the entire list is embedded in the outer list.

Adding Nonlist Elements

To return to CONS and APPEND, the two other primitives discussed in this section: We know that we can add a list element to the front of an existing list using CONS. For example:

    (CONS 'A '(B C D))

results in the list:

    (A B C D)

If we try the reverse of this:

    (CONS '(B C D) 'A)

we get a dotted list:

    ((B C D) . A)

APPEND is no help either, assuming that we wish to tack a nonlist object onto the end of an established list. The following use of APPEND

    (APPEND '(B C D) 'A)

also results in a dotted list:

    (B C D . A)

How do we add a nonlist element to the end of an established list without getting a dotted list? One answer is to use LIST in association with APPEND to convert the single character to a list:

    (APPEND '(B C D) (LIST 'A))

That is: Convert 'A to (A) and APPEND it to the list (B C D). The return is:

```
(B C D A)
```

This gives us a standard list, not a dotted list. You can also use LIST with the READ primitive (discussed in a later chapter) to construct standard lists from elements input via the microcomputer keyboard. LIST is a most valuable primitive; it allows the conversion of nonlist objects to bona fide lists for use with other primitives that require list arguments.

Caution: The LISP primitives CONS, APPEND, and LIST simply return lists that are products; they do not alter the value of any symbol that may represent a list or other object. Too often beginning LISP programmers think that:

```
(SETF X '(A B C))
(APPEND X '(D E F))
```

somehow alters the value of symbol X. It does not! Instead, the return from this use of APPEND is:

```
(A B C D E F)
```

The value of X remains the same:

```
(A B C)
```

APPEND does not alter the value symbol X represents. Changing a symbol's value requires SETF, SETQ, or other similar primitives.

We can use the list-building primitives to alter symbol values as a new list is built. But we will still need other primitives used specifically for assignment purposes. For example:

```
(SETF X '(A B C))
(SETF X (APPEND X '(D E F)))
```

In this example, the symbol X is initially assigned a value from the list:

```
(A B C)
```

SETF is then used to reassign X the list comprised of ' (D E F), which is appended to its current value. The new value of X is:

```
(A B C D E F G)
```

BASIC programmers should treat most LISP primitives as they treat BASIC functions. For instance, the use of the BASIC LEFT$

function in the following example does not change the value of its string argument, X$:

```
10 X$="HELLO"
20 PRINT LEFT$(X$,3)
```

If we write:

```
10 X$="HELLO"
20 X$=LEFT$(X$,3)
```

then we have made a change to X$ based upon the operation of LEFT$. But LEFT$ has still not altered the value; it has merely returned the left three characters in X$. In BASIC, the equally operator and not the function itself makes a value reassignment.

Use the list-building primitives to construct lists within their own function bodies. Each will return the combination it produces. However, this return value does not do anything to affect the arguments they are handed. The return can be used with other LISP primitives to perform tests (*predicates*—see Chapter 5) or to make assignments or reassignments, based upon the value of the return.

OTHER USEFUL PRIMITIVES

Common LISP is rich with primitives, special forms, and many other tools for efficient list programming. Some of these that are used quite often by LISP beginners are briefly discussed in this section.

VALUES

VALUES returns the values of all of its arguments. It is especially useful when you need to return a group of values from a procedure. The following example demonstrates the use of VALUES:

```
(SETF X 1)
(SETF Y 2)
(SETF Z 3)

(VALUES X Y Z)
```

This returns:

```
1
2
3
```

48

VALUES is often used as the return argument for user-programmed functions. Instead of returning a single value (as is the case with most functions), VALUES can return many.

BUTLAST

BUTLAST is aptly named: It returns a list comprised of all but the last element in its argument list. For example:

```
(BUTLAST '(A B C D E F G))
```

returns the list:

```
(A B C D E F)
```

BUTLAST might be thought of as REST in reverse (REST returns all but the first element of a list). BUTLAST can also be used with an optional argument to control the number of elements dropped from the return list. Thus:

```
(BUTLAST '(A B C D E F G H 1 2 3 4 5) 3)
```

returns the list:

```
(A B C D E F G H 1 2)
```

This is all but the last three elements of the former list. If the last (optional) argument had been 13 instead of 3, a NILL list would have been returned.

MAKE-LIST

MAKE-LIST is a handy function for making a list that contains a specified number of the same element. The function requires a positive integer value that specifies the number of elements in the list and a keyword (:INITIAL-ELEMENT) followed by the name of the element to be repeated. NIL is the default if the keyword option is not used; this generates a list comprised of the specified number of NIL's. The following example demonstrates the use of MAKE-LIST:

```
(MAKE-LIST 10 :INITIAL-ELEMENT 'Q)
```

This results in the list:

```
(Q Q Q Q Q Q Q Q Q Q)
```

which consists of the same ten elements, the symbol Q. If the keyword option had not been used, the list would have been:

```
(NIL NIL NIL NIL NIL NIL NIL NIL NIL NIL)
```

The keyword argument can be any object, such as:

```
(MAKE-LIST 3 :INITIAL-ELEMENT '(A B C))
```

This makes the list:

```
((A B C) (A B C) (A B C))
```

MEMBER

MEMBER is a Common LISP function that looks for a test element in a list argument. If the test element is found, LISP returns a list that contains all the items in the argument list, starting with the one that matched the test item. For example:

```
(MEMBER 'A '(A B C D E F G))
```

This returns:

```
(A B C D E F G)
```

because A is an element in the argument list. Since this is the first element, the entire list is returned. The next example returns a list containing only some of the elements in the original list:

```
(MEMBER 'D '(A B C D E F G))
```

This evaluation returns the list:

```
(D E F G)
```

That part of the original list argument that begins with the test element D is returned. MEMBER is a predicate and it will return NIL if it does not find a match in the argument list.

The LISP primitives discussed in this chapter are the ones most often used by the beginning LISP programmer. You should understand what each primitive does and how primitives interact. The more complex primitives are built from these basic tools of LISP.

Chapter 5

Predicates

In a LISP environment, a *predicate* is a procedure that tests for a condition and returns T when the specified condition is true and NIL when the condition is false. IF statement lines in BASIC also test for true and false conditions. For example:

IF X=Y THEN *Do something*

LISP compares values like this:

(= X Y)

In this example, if X is equal to Y, then T is returned. If the values represented by the two variable are not equal, then NIL is returned.

USING PREDICATES

ATOM

LISP offers many predicates that can be used to test constants and variable values. For example, ATOM tests an argument to determine whether it is an atom or a list. The following example demonstrates this predicate:

(ATOM 'HELLO)

The value T is returned because the argument ('HELLO) is, indeed, an atom. A true value is also returned by the following
example:

```
(ATOM 1234)
```

since all numbers are atoms. However,

```
(ATOM '(HELLO GOODBYE FAR))
```

returns NIL since the argument is a list and not an atom.

LISTP

As you might expect, LISP also has a predicate that tests an
argument to see if it is a list, returning T when it is and NIL when
it is not. This predicate is called LISTP (for list predicate) and it
is the reverse of ATOM. For example:

```
(LISTP '(HELLO GOODBYE FAR))
```

returns T, since the argument is a list and not an atom. T is also
returned in the following expression:

```
(LISTP '())
```

even though the argument is a NULL list. Note that LISTP does
not directly evaluate the contents of a list—it only tests for the presence of one. The following example returns NIL because the argument is an atom and not a list:

```
(LISTP 'HELLO)
```

Mathematical Predicates

You will recognize the following predicates as the standard
mathematical comparison symbols used in most computer
languages. They are:

```
(= X Y)
```

This returns T if X is equal to Y.

```
(> X Y)
```

This returns T if X is greater than Y.

```
(< X Y)
```

This returns T if X is less than Y.

```
(NULL X)
```

This returns T if X is a null list.

All but the last of these predicates can be used to compare more than two variables or values. In all cases comparisons are made on the entire contents of the argument, regardless of the number of values represented. For example:

```
(< 1 2 3 4 5 6 7 8 9)
```

returns T, since each number in the sequence from 0 to 9 is less than the number that follows it. Expressed in words, this predicate test says:

IF ONE IS LESS THAN TWO AND TWO IS LESS THAN THREE AND THREE IS LESS THAN FOUR AND FOUR IS LESS THAN FIVE AND FIVE IS LESS THAN SIX AND SIX IS LESS THAN SEVEN AND SEVEN IS LESS THAN EIGHT AND EIGHT IS LESS THAN NINE AND THEN RETURN T ELSE RETURN NIL.

What does the following expression evaluates to?

```
(< 1 2 3 4 5 6 7 6)
```

Every leading number is smaller than the one that follows except for the last two. Since the "less than" ($\setminus$) test does not prove true throughout the entire sequence, NIL is returned. The same operation can be applied to the "more then" (>) predicate and to the equality operator:

```
(= X Y Z)
```

In this example, if:

```
X=Y=Z
```

then a true value is returned, but if any variable is this three-variable argument is not equal to the others, NIL is returned.

Depending on the LISP programming package, many other predicates will be included. These may include the following:

```
(ZEROP X)
```

This returns T if X is equal to zero. (Note: X must be a number.)

```
(NUMBERP X)
```

This returns T if X represents a number.

```
(MINUSP X)
```

This returns T if X represents a negative value. (Note: X must be a number.)

```
(EVENP X)
```

This returns T if X represents an even number. (Note: X must be a number.)

These predicates are a standard part of Common LISP. If your LISP package does not include them, you will find it a simple matter to write your own specialized predicates as you become more acquainted with LISP programming.

BUILDING PREDICATES

Let's examine the methods used to build some simple LISP predicates. DEFUN will be used again, along with some of the simple predicates already provided by LISP. This combination can yield a large number of useful programming tools. We will begin by showing how the simple predicate ZEROP is constructed. This is already a part of most LISP interpreters but it makes a good first example. To create ZEROP you only need to build a predicate that determines if its argument is equal to zero. The predicate construction for ZEROP is:

```
(DEFUN ZEROP (ARG)
  (= ARG 0))
```

That's all there is to it. DEFUN defines the format of ZEROP. The first line shows us that the name of the predicate is ZEROP and that is expects one argument. The second line uses the standard LISP predicate for equality, the equal sign. From the previous discussion we know that the equality predicate returns T if its two arguments are equal and NIL if they are not. In this example, the equality predicate tests to see if ARG is equal to zero. (ARG was built using another LISP predicate.)

As another example, let's build a LISP predicate called TENP. TENP will return T if the argument is equal to ten and NIL if it is not. It is constructed as follows:

```
(DEFUN TENP (ARG)
 (= ARG 10))
```

This is almost identical to our ZEROP example, except the predicate name has been changed and ARG is tested against a different constant value. Another predicate can be used to see if the difference between two arguments is equal to ten as in:

```
(DEFUN TENMINUSP (ARG1 ARG2)
 (= (- ARG1 ARG2) 10))
```

The same basic arrangement is used to construct this predicate, although there is an additional mathematical operation. The format of the predicate is arranged so that it expects two arguments, ARG1 and ARG2. The equality predicate tests whether the value of its first argument is equal to the value of its second argument. The first argument is:

```
(- ARG1 ARG2)
```

The prefix notation calls for the subtraction of ARG2 from ARG1. Assuming a value of 30 for ARG1 and a value of 20 for ARG2, this expression evaluates to 10. The second part of the equality predicate's argument is the constant 10. Since 10 equals 10, a T is returned. Any other value for the first argument will result in a NIL return.

Now let's construct a predicate that returns T if a list contains three or more items. The predicate's construction follows:

```
(DEFUN LIST3 (ARG)
 (> (LENGTH ARG) 2))
```

Here the LENGTH primitive evaluates the number of objects in ARG (ARG represents the argument lists). The return value of this primitive is tested against the number 2 by the "more than" predicate. This results in a true T return if the LENGTH of the argument is 3 or more. If LENGTH ARG evaluates to 2 or less, NIL is returned.

TESTING NONNUMERIC OBJECTS

Until now, the great majority of the predicates we have discussed have used numeric constants or variables. But there are other predicates that deal specifically with lists or nonnumeric values. The equality predicate (=) tests numeric values only, therefore:

```
(= 'HELLO 'HELLO)
```

results in an error message. Common LISP offers the EQUAL predicate to test any type of object, be it numeric, list, or string. A string object is surrounded by quotation marks as in:

```
(SETQ X "hello")
```

The predicate STRINGP will test whether an object is indeed, a string rather than a number or a list. Thus:

```
(STRINGP X)
```

returns T if X represents a string value and NIL if it represents a list or a number.

Since so many different objects are associated with LISP, the EQUAL predicate is quite useful. Consider the following example:

```
(EQUAL X Y)
```

As long as X and Y represent the same quantity and type of object, a true T value is returned. This applies whether the variables represent numbers, lists, strings, etc. For example:

```
(EQUAL 'HELLO 'HELLO)
(EQUAL 10 10)
(EQUAL '(A B C) '(A B C))
```

In each of these examples, a true value is returned by the predicate EQUAL. In most versions of Common LISP, EQUAL has several counterparts that allow special test evaluations of various arguments.

LOGICAL OPERATORS

LISP's logical operators are often referred to as *logical predicates*. They include AND, NOT, and OR.

The NOT predicate returns T (true) if and only if its argument value is the logical value NIL. We can use NOT to test for null (empty) lists as in the following example:

```
(SETQ X ' ( ) )
(NOT X).
```

First, variable X is set to a value of the null list [()]. Next, the NOT predicate determines if the contents of X represent a null value or NIL. This example returns a true value because X represents a NIL value. If these were not the case, a NIL value would have been returned.

The AND predicate evaluates its arguments from left to right on a one-by-one basis. If any of the arguments evaluate to NIL then NIL is immediately returned and no further evaluation occurs. If *all* arguments evaluate to true, then a true value is returned by this predicate. For example:

```
(AND ' (A B) ' (A B C) ' ( ) )
```

returns a NIL value because the last argument is a null list. Since one of the arguments evaluates to NIL, NIL is returned. The following example returns a true value because no argument evaluates to NIL:

```
(AND ' (A B) ' (A B C) ' (A B C D))
```

The AND predicate is useful for testing large groups of objects that may have an object that must evaluate to NIL.

The same is true of the OR predicate. It is used to test forms or arguments. "OR" returns a true value if only one of the arguments evaluates to a non-NIL value. Evaluation stops as soon as a value other than NIL occurs. Here is an example of the OR predicate:

```
(OR ' ( ) ' ( ) ' (A B) )
```

The return value of this example is true because the last argument evaluates to a non-NIL value.

Predicates are used in Common LISP as they are in other computer languages. Predicates test for a certain condition or conditions and return one of two possible values, depending on the outcome of each test. In LISP, the values are T for a test that proves true and NIL for a test that proves false.

Chapter 6

Input and Output

Receiving information from the keyboard and writing information to the monitor screen are a cinch using Common LISP. The BASIC language programmer will see only a few minor changes from what he/she has used in a BASIC environment.

Input and output are handled by two Common LISP primitives appropriately named READ and PRINT. READ obviously reads information from the keyboard. PRINT is roughly similar to the BASIC PRINT statement in that it writes information to the monitor screen. Several other LISP primitives perform similar functions in slightly different formats, but we will concentrate mainly on the primitives READ and PRINT.

THE READ PRIMITIVE

The primitive READ is the LISP equivalent of BASIC's INPUT statement. Both allow information to be received from the main input device, which is usually the keyboard. Using READ, keyboard input can be processed, assigned to a variable, or trigger other processor actions.

READ's simplest use is to return whatever is input at the keyboard. For example:

(READ) *type something*<CR>

evaluates to or returns "Type something," which was input from the keyboard. BASIC programmers will immediately notice that there is no variable to "hold" what was typed. Upon pressing the carriage return key, READ automatically displays the keyboard information on the screen.

How do we assign keyboard input to a variable? We can demonstrate this by duplicating the following BASIC program in LISP:

```
10 INPUT X
```

Admittedly, this portion of a BASIC program does nothing useful. The example uses the BASIC statement INPUT to halt program execution until input is received from the keyboard. When the carriage return key is pressed, numeric variable X is assigned the value of the keyboard input. If we type 44 in response to the BASIC INPUT prompt(?), variable X will equal to 44.

To accomplish the same program function in LISP, the following procedure can be used:

```
(SETF X (READ))
```

As we have already discussed, SETF is a primitive that assigns variables. It requires two arguments, the first of which is a symbol (a *variable*, in BASIC terminology). The second argument can be another assigned symbol, a constant, or any procedure that returns a value. The example uses READ as the second argument to SETF. We can also say that the keyboard input serves as the argument to SETF. When this procedure is executed, X will be equal to the keyboard input.

The BASIC program example required the input value to be numeric rather than a string. In LISP this is not a required or at least not in the program example shown. Whatever is typed at the keyboard—a number, a list, a string—will be symbol X's value.

The READ primitive is as versatile as the other LISP primitives and it is used with these to develop lists partially or entirely comprised of keyboard input information. In the example:

```
(SETF X (LIST (READ) (READ) (READ)))
```

X is assigned the combined input of the three READ primitives. The LIST primitive incorporates the READ primitives into a single list.

BASIC programmers know that INPUT does not allow a comma when obtaining a string input. In LISP, READ automatically terminates the keyboard read sequence upon receiving a space. This is found in many languages. In the above procedure, you could type:

ONE< space bar > TWO < space bar >THREE< CR >

and X would equal:

(ONE TWO THREE)

You can even replace the carriage return with another space and get the same result. The keyboard action of the READ primitive is closely duplicated by the following BASIC program:

```
10 A$=INKEY$
20 IF A$=CHR$(13) OR A$=CHR$(32)
        THEN 50
30 X$=X$+A$
40 GOTO 10
50 END
```

In this example X$ represents what would be the return value of READ in LISP.

READ automatic termination of a keyboard read operation only occurs when standard objects are input; it does not apply when the keyboard input begins with an open parenthesis. This would be standard if an entire list were input like this:

(READ)

Keyboard response:

(HELLO GOODBYE FAR) <CR> or <space>

READ returns:

(HELLO GOODBYE FAR)

The keyboard read terminates upon receiving the carriage return or a space because neither lie within a list body (i.e., within parentheses).

Building Lists with READ

Let's assume that we want to build a list using elements typed in via the keyboard. We first need to determine whether the list is to be composed of individual elements, embedded lists, or even a mixture of the two. As an easy beginning example, we will select a standard list like (A B C), which has no embedded lists.

The easiest way to build the list is to use READ with the LISP primitive LIST. As you will remember, LIST forms a single list from its arguments, which can be any object. The following use of LIST and READ gives the desired results:

```
(LIST (READ) (READ) (READ))
```

This example assumes that you want to build a list containing three elements, each input from the keyboard. Therefore, if the keyboard input is:

```
A  <space>  B  <space>  C  <CR>
```

the returned list is:

```
(A B C)
```

Just what we were after.

this list could be assigned to a symbol:

```
(SETF X (LIST (READ) (READ) (READ)))
```

The symbol X now equates to the list (A B C). However, X will equate to any three items typed in, so the list does not have to be (A B C).

APPEND can add lists to one that currently exists, as the following example shows:

```
(APPEND ' (A B C)
             (LIST (READ) (READ) (READ)))
```

With the following keyboard input:

```
D  <space>  E  <space>  F  <CR>
```

the return is:

```
(A B C D E F)
```

The LIST primitive is included in the example for convenience, for the exercise can also be written as:

```
(APPEND ' (A B C) (READ) (READ) (READ))
```

Which gives the same returned list *if* the keyboard input data are input as lists:

(D) <space> (E) <space > (F) <CR>

Each input element is a list; if we use the original input:

D <space> E <space> F <CR>

the returned list reads:

(A B C . F)

The first two inputs are ignored by APPEND, because all arguments to APPEND must be lists (except for the last argument, which can be any object). Without the parentheses signifying lists, only the last product of READ is appended to the first list argument and the dotted list occurs. Always be aware of the types of objects returned by READ and other input primitives; you should also be aware of the types of arguments required by primitives that may use keyboard input.

Remember that either a space bar <space> or a carriage return <CR> triggers the end of the keyboard read operation. Neither of these characters are a part of the value that READ returns.

A Simple I/O Loop

The previous examples used a series of READs to build lists of predetermined sizes. We can take a clue from the next chapter on LISP loops and use the READ primitive to build lists of predetermined sizes with a little more ease.

The following BASIC program gives an idea of what we will be trying to accomplish in LISP:

```
10 FOR X=1 TO 10
20 INPUT A$
30 PRINT A$
40 NEXT X
```

This simple program allows the input of keyboard information and assigns it to the string variable A$. This value is then displayed on the screen.

A LISP-equivalent program is:

```
(DO ((X 1 (+ 1 X)))
    ((> X 10))
    (SETF A (READ))
    (PRINT A))
```

This program is quite inefficient, but suffices for demonstration purposes. The LISP symbol, X, is the equivalent of variable X in the BASIC program example. The same applies to A$ and A in BASIC and LISP, respectively. In this LISP program, X is assigned an initial value of 1, it is stepped in increments of one as the loop cycles. The exit sequence tests whether X is more than 10. On each loop pass, SETF assigns A the value input from the keyboard. Each time READ is encountered the loop's execution temporarily halts until READ returns a carriage return or a space. PRINT then displays the value of A on the monitor screen.

Again, this is a most inefficient program, but so was the BASIC program example. But in BASIC we cannot write:

```
10 FOR X=1 TO 10
20 PRINT INPUT
```

we are not restricted from doing this in Common LISP. The following example is a more efficient rendition of the previous LISP program:

```
(DO ((X 1 (+ 1 X)))
    ((> X 10))
    (PRINT (READ)))
```

We have now eliminated the assignment line completely.

Suppose we want to set up a looping keyboard READ that terminates only when instructed to do so, presumably from a keyboard signal? In BASIC, we could write:

```
10 WHILE A$ <> "END"
20 INPUT A$
30 IF A$="END" THEN 50
40 PRINT A$
50 WEND
```

LISP simulates this with the following method:

```
(DO ((A (READ) (SETF A (READ))))
    ((EQUAL A 'END))
    (PRINT A))
```

We don't even need to use a conditional, because the DO loop checks for termination before PRINT is executed. Both the BASIC and LISP examples use "END" or 'END as the exit command instead of displaying it on the screen.

With these examples in mind, let's build a list from keyboard input using a DO loop, READ, and some list-building primitives discussed earlier:

```
(DO ((A (LIST (READ))
        (APPEND A (LIST (READ))))))
    ((EQUAL (LAST A) '(END)) A)
    (PRINT A))
```

Initially A is set to the value of the keyboard input using READ. On each pass of the loop, READ is accessed. LIST always accompanies READ in this example because we want a standard list of elements comprised of the keyboard input; otherwise, we would get a dotted list. A uses APPEND to add (LIST (READ)) to the existing value of A. The exit sequence uses LAST to check for the presence of END as the last loop element.

Since we know the type of list this procedure produces and since we assume the input of nonlist data from the keyboard (i.e., no parentheses surrounding objects), it is safe to use LAST for this check. Notice that the exit element is displayed as a LIST (END) rather than as the nonlist object 'END.

With the keyboard input of **HELLO**, **GOODBYE**, **FAR**, and **END**, the screen *will* display:

```
(HELLO)
(HELLO GOODBYE)
(HELLO GOODBYE FAR)
(HELLO GOODBYE FAR END)
```

before the loop terminates.

It is through procedures such as these that programs are heavily user-integrated. The contents of lists whereby the elements are supplied by the program user at the keyboard can be used to determine many, many things based upon comparing these elements with other lists. This is the way artificial intelligence applications are written, although this example is very simple; and only a miniscule part of that required even to begin to emulate human intelligence.

As you can see from the example, END is a part of the list. This is often undesirable, so we can delete it using the following rewrite:

```
(DO ((A (LIST (READ))
        (APPEND A (LIST (READ))))))
    ((EQUAL (LAST A) '(END)) X)
    (SETF X A))
```

The program now returns the value of symbol X instead of the value of A. On each pass of the loop, SETF sets the value of X to that of A. However, when the exit input ('END) is provided at the keyboard, the loop is exited *before* SETF is called again. This results in a return value that includes all but the last keyboard input. There are other ways to do this, but this method is easy to understand and works efficiently.

We can also write a function that accepts input from the keyboard and builds a list that can be used for many different programming applications:

```
(DEFUN INP-LIST-TIL-END ()
  (DO ((A (LIST (READ))
          (APPEND A (LIST (READ)))))
      ((EQUAL (LAST A) '(END)) X)
      (SETF X A)))
```

With this personal function, procedures like:

```
(SETF Y (INP-LIST-TIL-END))
```

Greatly simplify data entry. To make the function a bit fancier, it is a simple matter to add an automatic prompt:

```
(DEFUN INP-LIST-TIL-END ()
  (PRINT
   '(Input a list element <type END to quit>))
  (DO ((A (LIST (READ))
          (APPEND A (LIST (READ)))))
      ((EQUAL (LAST A) '(END)) X)
      (SETF X A)
      (PRINT
       '(Input a list element <type END to quit>))))
```

Now whenever this function is called, it will tell the user what it expects in the way of arguments (keyboard input) and prompt the user about the exit procedure.

SIMPLE PRINTING

So far we have only touched upon the subject of output. The PRINT primitive outputs information to the monitor and is similar to the PRINT statement in BASIC. But, there is more to PRINT than meets the eye.

When PRINT is evoked, it doesn't simply print its argument. First, it prints a new line character, also known as a carriage return. Then its argument is written to the monitor screen. But PRINT isn't finished yet. Following the screen write, PRINT also writes a space. For example:

```
(PRINT 'HELLO)
```

results in the screen write:

```
<CR>
```

HELLO <space>

This is the formatting PRINT displays each time it is called. PRINT has already been used in this chapter to write the output of loops to the monitor screen.

If you do not want the built-in formatting of PRINT (i.e., the leading carriage return and the trailing space), you can use another output primitive called PRIN1. This function also writes its argument to the screen, but without the leading carriage return and trailing space.

To demonstrate the differences, the following programs are set up as continuous loops:

(LOOP (PRINT 'HELLO))

and

(LOOP (PRIN1 'HELLO))

The first example uses PRINT while the second loops uses PRIN1. The screen write produced by the first is:

```
HELLO
HELLO
HELLO
HELLO
```
        (continues . . .)

The second loop using PRIN1 produces:

HELLOHELLOHELLOHELLOHELLOHELLO ...

The first example shows the effect of PRINT's built-in carriage return. For most purposes this is convenient, but PRIN1 is useful when you want the screen print format to be programmer controlled.

Using PRIN1, a suitable horizontal screen format can be set up simply by including the necessary spaces following each word grouping:

(LOOP (PRIN1 'HELLO)

Notice that there is a space between the O in HELLO and the closing parenthesis. This space acts like another character preceded by the single quote.

When this example is executed, the screen displays:

HELLO HELLO HELLO HELLO HELLO HELLO

This method thus provides the necessary spacing between words to present a pleasing display.

Of course, you may have to call for a carriage return. This can be done by using PRIN1 to display horizontal information on the screen and then using PRINT when a new line is to be started.

TERPRI and PRINC

Common Lisp also offers another output primitive called TER-PRI. TERPRI simply outputs a new-line character (carriage return) and returns NIL. Using TERPRI is the same as typing a carriage return. BASIC programmers will find TERPRI the same as:

```
10 PRINT CHR$(13)
```

Using TERPRI along with PRIN1 provides a more versatile set of formatting tools for simple printing operations. However, we are still quite limited if all we had to depend upon were these simple output primitives.

There is another primitive for displaying information on the monitor screen. It is called PRINC and it works just like PRIN1 except that its output contains no escape sequences. PRINC is said to make a nicer screen display than the output from PRIN1, which contains those escape characters that make it acceptable to other functions.

One prime example of the difference between PRINC's and PRIN1's screen display is demonstrated in the following example:

```
(PRIN1 "HELLO")
```

results in:

```
"HELLO"
```

while

```
(PRINC "HELLO")
```

produces

```
HELLO
```

As you can see, PRIN1 (like print) displays its string argument with the surrounding double quotes. PRINC drops the double quotes. While the latter's output is more pleasing to the eye, PRIN1 and PRINT's output readily identifies the object as a string, whereas PRINC's output does not.

FORMAT

Fortunately, Common Lisp offers a very versatile function that can perform a myriad of complex (or simple) screen writes. FOR-

68

MAT allows the programmer to set up complex screen write formats in a fairly easy manner. C language programmers will find many comparisons between Common LISP's FORMAT primitive and C's **printf** function.

FORMAT is used in the following form:

(FORMAT <*destination-control*> *arguments*)

The format is fairly simple, although the destination-control reference may seem a bit strange. Destination-control is an argument that tells LISP where to display the arguments that follow. If we use T for the destination, LISP selects standard output, that is, the monitor screen. Other arguments write the information to a file or even to a symbol. For now we will use T to write the arguments to the monitor screen.

The following example uses FORMAT in its most simple form:

(FORMAT T "Gone with the wind.")

This displays the contents of the quoted string argument on the screen and returns NIL. FORMAT returns NIL after it completes its operation. This is a normal occurrence. The FORMAT example is closely equivalent to:

(PRINT "Gone with the wind.")

FORMAT does not display the enclosing quotes of the argument string; PRINT does.

So far FORMAT has not shown us anything entirely new, but this will change with the next example. Assume that we want to print a phrase followed by the value of a symbol. A BASIC program example is:

```
10 X=10
20 PRINT "THE VALUE IS";X
```

This program prints the phrase:

THE VALUE IS 10

on the monitor screen. To do this in LISP, we can use:

```
(SETF X 10)
(PRIN1 "THE VALUE IS ")
(PRIN1 X)
```

FORMAT can make this job much more simple:

```
(SETF X 10)
(FORMAT T "THE VALUE IS ~D" X)
```

This will look a bit odd to BASIC programmers, but C programmers should feel right at home, because this LISP example is equivalent to the C line:

```
printf("THE VALUE IS %d", x)
```

assuming that variable *x* is equal to 10.

Format Directives

FORMAT is invaluable because it can accept what are known as *format directives*. These are represented by the tilde character (~) followed by a single character that represents the type of directive. In the LISP example above, the tilde was followed by the character D. This tells FORMAT to expect an integer (a whole number with no trailing decimal point). FORMAT replaces D with the argument that follows the quoted string. In this example the argument is represented by the symbol X, but we could just as easily have replaced X with the number 10.

Note: If the argument supplied (X in this example) is not an integer, then the true argument value is displayed. In other words, if you use:

```
(FORMAT T ("THE VALUE IS   D" 4.555))
```

then 4.555 is displayed as if it were printed by PRIN1. The D directive applies only to integer values; if you use a list or some other nonnumeric object for the argument to this directive, the object is displayed as if used with PRIN1.

C programmers take heed: unlike **printf**, the format directives supplied to FORMAT do not perform conversions. However, some conversions are possible. The following example demonstrates one:

```
(FORMAT T
  "The hexadecimal equivalent of 255 is  X." 255)
```

This displays:

```
The hexadecimal equivalent of 255 is FF.
```

The X directive used with FORMAT tells FORMAT to expect an integer argument and then convert it to hexadecimal format. FF represents the decimal number 255 in hexadecimal notation, so FORMAT has properly performed the conversion. If any argument but an integer is supplied, the value of this argument will be displayed and it will not be converted to hexadecimal format.

Octal formatting of integers is also possible with FORMAT:

```
(FORMAT T
"The octal equivalent of 255 is  O." 255)
```

FORMAT displays:

The octal equivalent of 255 IS 377.

You even can convert integer arguments to 8-bit binary equivalents using the B directive as in:

```
(FORMAT T
"The binary equivalent of 255 is  B." 255)
```

This produces

11111111

which represents 255 as a binary number.

Another important directive is S, which displays its argument as if it were used with PRIN1. Here is an example of this usage:

```
(FORMAT T "A  S is an animal." 'horse)
```

This displays the message:

A horse is an animal.

Notice that it doesn't matter where the directives are placed, so long as they are a part of the quoted string argument. We can also mix and match directives in the same quoted control line:

```
(FORMAT T
"  D IS THE  S OF  D." 144 'SQUARE 12)
```

This displays:

144 is the square of 12

The arguments following the quoted string are accessed in order by the directives. In other words, the arguments that follow the quoted string must be in order, because the first directive will access the first argument, the second directive will access the second argument, and so on.

If you try these examples using a LISP interpreter, you will notice that the screen write starts as soon as the sample lines are input and that no carriage return is executed before the phrase is written. Your write may look like this:

```
(FORMAT T "Print  S." 'HELLO)HELLO
NIL
```

The NIL return is normal as is the entire screen write, but it would look far better if the screen write began on the next line. A carriage return and a line feed command, better known as a "new line", will do this. FORMAT offers a new line directive that accomplishes this taste. It is demonstrated below:

```
(FORMAT T
" %  I have generated a new line.")
```

The directive for a new line is   % and it requires no argument. The above example should look like this on your monitor screen:

```
(FORMAT T
" % I have generated a new line.")
I have generated a new line.
NIL
```

The new line directive automatically executes a carriage return and line feed. Notice that the "I" in the message is indented one character from the left edge. This occurred because a space preceded the same letter in the quoted control string. The space was left in order to accentuate the use of the new line directive, but it is not necessary to space between directives and other portions of the quoted line, even if two directives are placed back to back.

FORMAT is a very complex function. The full Common LISP version is not always totally supported by all Common LISP programming packages, but all of them usually include enough of FORMAT's features to make this the most used function for text formatting.

OTHER I/O FEATURES

Although we have discussed the basic input/output capabilities of Common LISP, there are many more that are variations of the basic functions. Some of these are briefly reviewed in the following pages.

The Y-OR-N-P Function

A very useful function, weirdly named Y-OR-N-P (for Yes-or-No Predicate), uses both the input and output of the microcomputer to handle user responses. It can be used as simply as in:

```
(Y-OR-N-P)
```

which displays the screen prompt:

```
(Y or N)
```

This function is a predicate that is "True" if the user types in an upper-or lowercase 'Y'. If an upper-or lowercase 'N' is typed in, then the function returns NIL. If any other character is typed in, the prompt repeats itself, requesting either a 'Y' or an 'N' response.

This is a handy function because the return value can be tested for T or NIL and appropriate actions can be taken based upon this return. No error trapping is necessary to guard against an improper input response since the function does this for you.

However Y-OR-N-P even goes further. It also prints prompts to explain to the user, what he/she is to respond to. For instance:

```
(Y-OR-N-P "Do you wish to continue?")
```

displays:

```
Do you wish to continue? (Y or N)
```

Execution if the program temporarily halts until either of the two appropriate responses is received from the keyboard.

This function acts like a combination of FORMAT and READ. The prompt messages are handled like those used with FORMAT. It accepts format directives as in following example: demonstrates:

```
(Y-OR-N-P "Is your name  S?" (Frederick).
```

This displays:

```
Is your name (Frederick)? (Y or N)
```

Y-OR-N-P can be used like other predicates. The following example incorporates it in the exit clause of a DO loop:

```
(DO ((X 1 (+ 1 X)))
    ((Y-OR-N-P "Do you wish to stop?"))
    (PRINT X))
```

Each time the loop cycles, a check of the exit clause is made and the prompt is generated. As long as the user types 'N' or 'n', the loop will continue to cycle and the value of symbol X will be displayed on the monitor. Responding 'Y' or 'y' returns a true (T) value and the DO loop terminates.

Common LISP also offers a similar function, YES-OR-NO-P. This performs exactly like the previous function, except the initial prompt line is:

```
(Yes or No)
```

The user must type one of these two options to bring about a T or NIL return. Any other keyboard response results in the re-printing the message. You must hit the carriage return key to return from this prompt.

READ-LINE

The Common LISP READ-LINE function works similarly to READ, but it does not exit after receiving a space bar hit. This is true even if the space character occurs outside a set of parentheses. Read-Line also returns a character string as its object. The following example demonstrates READ-LINE:

```
(READ-LINE)
```

Keyboard input:

```
Now is the time.
```

Return:

```
"Now is the time."
```

READ-CHAR

READ-CHAR works like READ but exits after a single key has been pressed. This function returns the ASCII code of the key that was hit during its read cycle.

Common LISP has many variations to the basic READ and PRINT functions. There are simple functions that can be combined to create complex functions such as FORMAT. In LISP there are many ways to read and write characters and to format them. Receiving information from the keyboard and writing information to the screen is done easily with PRINT and READ, but there are other functions that may serve even better. The idea is to get to know the properties and limitations of each function. You can then decide just which Common Lisp input/output functions are best for any given programming assignment.

Chapter 7

Lisp Loops

In BASIC the FOR-NEXT-STEP loop is an integral program structure used to execute one or more program lines until the exit value is reached. BASIC also offers the WHILE-WEND loop that is (unfortunately) used less often by the average BASIC programmer. I say unfortunately, because WHILE-WEND loop can often be used to better advantage, such as preventing the overuse of the GOTO statement, which tends to cloud the programmer's intentions.

Those who program in other high-level languages tend to use the equivalents of WHILE-WEND loops far more often than the FOR-NEXT-STEP equivalents. In the C programming language, for instance, the programmer has a choice of "while" and "for" loops. Often, "for" loops are inserted in the body of a "while" loop, the latter containing any number of program routines. In C (as in many other languages), there is also a "do" loop that is used far less often than the other two.

In Common LISP, the "do" loop is most often used for *iteration*. This term may be foreign to you, but you have used iteration many times in writing programs, regardless of the program's language. *Interation* is the repetition of an action or procedure in program loop.

The "do" loop is similar to C's "while" loop, but "while" tests for the exit condition at the loop's top or beginning; do loops check for this condition at the bottom.

Fortunately, we can use a "do" loop in LISP to replace BASIC's FOR-NEXT-STEP loop or WHILE-WEND loop. Beginning LISP programmers seem to find the actions of the "do" loop difficult to understand, especially if they are also BASIC programmers.

For a clear explanation of the LISP "do" loop, let's first examine the following BASIC program:

```
10 FOR X=1 TO 25 STEP 1
20 PRINT X
30 NEXT X
```

This simple BASIC program uses the FOR-NEXT STEP loop to increment the value of variable X from 1 to 25 in steps of 1. The second program line prints the value of X to the monitor screen. The last line recycles the loop as long as X is not more than 25.

The direct equivalent of this in a LISP "do" loop is:

```
(DO ((X 1 (+ 1 X)))
    ((> X 25))
    (PRINT X))
```

In plain English, this procedure says:

1. Assign X an initial value of 1.
2. Increment X by 1.
3. If X is more than 25, exit the loop.
4. While looping, print the value of X.

Let's examine the first line:

```
(DO ((X 1 (+ 1 X)))
```

First, DO indicates the loop. The starting and step values are assigned; the notation (X 1 (+ 1 X) means the same as X = 1 STEP 1.

The second line describes the exit sequence. In the BASIC program example, we know that X can equal as much as 25, but with LISP we use the "more-than" predicate:

```
((> X 25))
```

This means that the loop is exited when X is greater than 25 or equal to 26. If we used:

```
((= X 25))
```

then the loop would exit too soon. Why? Look at the LISP procedure again. Notice that PRINT X is the last line of the procedure. PRINT

X is executed after the exit sequence has been evaluated. Therefore, ((= X 25)) would result in a true return (T) and cause the loop to exit before the loop action was taken. This procedure would print the values 1 through 24 on the screen instead of 1 through 25 as intended.

Here is another BASIC program example:

```
10 FOR X=1 TO 20 STEP 1
20 Y = X + 1
30 PRINT X
40 PRINT Y
50 NEXT X
```

This is another simple FOR-NEXT-STEP loop that contains several statements within the loop body. The LISP equivalent is:

```
(DO ((X 1 (+ 1 X)))
    ((> X 20))
    (SETQ Y (+ X 1))
    (PRINT X)
    (PRINT Y))
```

All the procedures following the exit sequence are properly executed. You do not need to enclose the loop actions within a looping framework as in BASIC. The first two lines of the procedure form the complete loop. All the lines that follow represent procedures that are carried out in the body of the loop.

NESTED LOOPS

Nesting "do" loops in LISP is quite simple, once you understand the basic workings of this form of iteration. A BASIC example as follows:

```
10 FOR X=1 TO 20 STEP 1
20 FOR Y=1 TO 5 STEP 1
30 PRINT X
40 PRINT Y
50 NEXT Y
60 NEXT X
```

The outer loop of this simple program, represented by variable X, contains an inner or nested loop represented by variable Y. Every time the outer loop cycles, the nested loop is repeated in its entirety. The program nested accesses the loop 20 times because of the top value of the outer loop is 20.

The following is the LISP equivalent of this BASIC program:

```
(DO ((X 1 (+ 1 X)))
    ((> X 20))
    (DO ((Y 1 (+ 1 Y)))
        ((> Y 5))
        (PRINT X)
        (PRINT Y)))
```

Notice that the nested loop is treated like any other procedure inserted into the outer loop. The outer loop contains only a single object: the inner loop. The following example increases the number of actions carried out by the outer loop in our initial BASIC program:

```
10 FOR X=1 TO 20 STEP 1
20 PRINT"OUTSIDE LOOP"
30 PRINT"STARTING INSIDE LOOP"
40 FOR Y=1 TO 5 STEP 1
50 PRINT"INSIDE INNER LOOP"
60 NEXT Y
70 NEXT X
```

The LISP equivalent is:

```
(DO ((X 1 (+ 1 X)))
    ((> X 20))
    (PRINT '(OUTSIDE LOOP))
    (PRINT '(STARTING INSIDE LOOP))
    (DO ((Y 1 (+ 1 Y)))
        ((> Y 5))
        (PRINT '(INSIDE INNER LOOP))))
```

Each LISP example uses the PRINT primitive to show the results of the loop cycle on the monitor screen, but it is a simple matter to make a "do" loop to return a certain value or evaluation prompt upon loop termination. The following example demonstrates this:

```
(DO ((X 1 (+ 1 X)))
    ((> X 20) Y)
    (SETQ Y (* X 2)))
```

The change from the other LISP example is in the second line that evaluates the return sequence. When X is more than 20, the value of Y is returned. The last line sets the value of Y at two times the value of X. Because Y is incremented as the loop cycles, this procedure returns a value of 40, which is two times the exit value of X.

The preceding discussion and examples have shown how the

"do" loop in LISP can simulate BASIC's FOR-NEXT-STEP loop. But what about WHILE-WEND loops? After all, these loops do not step a value handed to the statement itself. The WHILE-WEND loop simply cycles until a specified expression in the body of the loop proves true. The following BASIC program is an example:

```
10 WHILE Y * 2 < 200
20 Y = Y * 10
30 WEND
```

This program works the formula $Y = 1 + Y * 10$ over and over until the value of $Y * 2$ equals or exceeds the exit test-value of 200. The LISP equivalent is:

```
(DO ((Y 0 (* Y 10)))
    ((OR (= (* Y 2) 200) (> Y 200))))
```

In English this procedure says, "Do $Y = 1 + Y * 10$ until 2 times Y is equal to or more than 200. This can also be expressed by the BASIC program:

```
10 FOR Y=0 TO 1000000' (INFINITY)
20 Y=Y+1*10
30 IF Y>200 THEN 50
40 NEXT Y
50 ' (NEW ROUTINE UPON LOOP EXIT)
```

Neither of these programs prints any information to the screen, but they do show how a WHILE-WEND loop can be simulated using LISP's "do" loop procedure.

EXITING A LOOP

Each of these examples has used a mathematical formula or sequence as part of the loop. How can we set up the LISP equivalent of:

```
10 WHILE A$<>"END"
20 INPUT A$
30 PRINT A$
40 WEND
```

This BASIC program allows string information to be input from the keyboard each time the loop cycles. This information is then reprinted. When the input is equal to "END," the loop is exited.

There are several ways of doing this in LISP using a "do" loop. For instance:

```
(SETQ A)
(DO ((Q 1 (+ 1 Q)))
    ((EQUAL A 'END))
    (SETQ A (READ))
    (PRINT A))
```

Initially, SETQ declares A a symbol. In this case, no value is assigned to A. Therefore, it is equal to NIL. This step is necessary to avoid an error message. The "do" loop uses symbol Q as a count variable, but the loop exit does not depend on the value of Q. The exit routine is triggered when A is equal to "END." This procedure can also be written as:

```
(SETQ A)
(DO ((Q 1))
    ((EQUAL A 'END))
    (SETQ A (READ))
    (PRINT A))
```

Here no step value for Q is supplied and none is necessary. Q simple remains equal to one and the value of A determines the loop exit condition as before.

The same procedure can even be written as:

```
(SETQ A)
(DO ((X))
    ((EQUAL A 'END))
    (SETQ A (READ))
    (PRINT A))
```

In this example, no starting value is specifically assigned to X, so X is therefore equal to NIL. In the "do" loop, a sequence of:

```
(DO ((X 1)))
```

is the equivalent of:

```
(DO ((SETQ X 1))
```

(the SETQ primitive is assumed).

MULTIPLE LOOP VARIABLES

In BASIC it is sometimes necessary to use a loop to increment additional variables. We usually do this with a FOR-NEXT loop and increment variables within the loop body as in the following example:

```
10 FOR X=1 TO 10
20 Y=X+1
30 Z=X+2
40 PRINT X
50 PRINT Y
60 PRINT Z
70 NEXT X
```

This loop increments three different variables to three different
values, each of which is dependent upon the value of X, the main
loop variable.

We can duplicate this program in LISP with the following procedure:

```
(DO ((X 1 (+ 1 X)))
    ((> X 10))
    (SETQ Y (+ X 1))
    (SETQ Z (+ X 2))
    (PRINT X)
    (PRINT Y)
    (PRINT Z))
```

This yields the same results as the BASIC program.

LISP offers us the advantage of naming more than one loop
variable and incrementing each loop variable as a separate entity.
This is different from depending on a single loop variable whose
value is added or subtracted to other variables. The following procedure is equivalent to the LISP example above:

```
(DO ((X 1 (+ 1 X))
     (Y 1 (+ 2 Y))
     (Z 1 (+ 3 Z))
    ((> X 10))
    (PRINT X)
    (PRINT Y)
    (PRINT Z))
```

The sequence that makes up the first three lines of this procedure
names three separate symbols and increments them individually
each time the loop cycles. Don't think that the symbols Y and Z
constitute nested loops—they do not! These are just extra variables
incremented as part of the loop cycle.

Incrementing through Lists

Unlike BASIC, LISP does not restrict us to numeric variables
for loop counts. A loop like this in BASIC:

```
FOR A$=B$ to C$
```

would result in an error message. LISP is not so touchy. For
example:

```
(SETQ E '(HELLO GOODBYE FAR))
(DO ((X E (REST X)))
    ((EQUAL X NIL))
    (PRINT X))
```

Symbol E is initially equal to the list (HELLO GOODBYE FAR).
In the loop, symbol X is initially set to the value of E, but the step
portion of the loop construction says to increment X by (REST X)
(i.e., the value of X minus the first element in its list). The above
procedure prints the following to the monitor screen:

```
(HELLO GOODBYE FAR)
(GOODBYE FAR)
(FAR)
```

This procedure might be thought of as deincrementing the elements
in the list. Notice that no numerical values are used in this procedure.

Now let's build a procedure that will allow us to construct a
single list composed entirely of elements input at the keyboard. The
list is completed when the last keyboard input is "END":

```
(DO ((X (LIST (READ))
        (APPEND X (LIST (READ)))))
    ((EQUAL (LAST X) '(END)))
    (PRINT X))
```

This function builds a single list by first assigning symbol X the
value of the first keyboard input. With each loop cycle, additional
keyboard input is appended to the current list contained in X. The
LIST primitive returns the keyboard input as a list. APPEND concatenates each list handed to it by the LIST/READ combination.
APPEND requires that all arguments handed to it be lists, except
for the last item, which can be any object. The PRINT primitive
displays the growing list on the screen. Thus the list represented
by X is incremented by each successive list typed in at the keyboard.

This is an efficient way to use a "do" loop, although there are
many other ways of accomplishing the same operation. The "do"
loop is a relatively new addition to LISP. At one time PROG was
used for such operations, because it was the only primitive available
to create explicit loops before the addition of the "do" loop. PROG
is considered outmoded in Common LISP, so it will not be discussed
in this chapter.

DOTIMES

DOTIMES is a variation of DO. It is easier to use than DO if you only need a loop that will exit after a stated number of cycles. Its format is:

```
(DOTIMES (VAR NUM RETURN)
         (CONTENTS)
```

where VAR is the loop variable, NUM is the number of loop cycles, RETURN is the result to be returned upon exit, and CONTENTS is any forms to be looped. The following example demonstrates DOTIMES:

```
(DOTIMES (X 10 'T)
         (PRINT X))
```

DOTIMES prints the value of X, its loop variable:

```
0
1
2
3
4
5
6
7
8
9
T
```

The loop automatically assigns the variable a starting value of 0 and the count maximum is used with an internal ($<$) predicate, so the loop does not terminate as long as the loop variable is less than the total count number. True (T) is returned, because the RESULT tested for was 'T. This could have been something like:

```
(DOTIMES (X 10 (/ X 2))
```

for a return of 4.5 in this example.

DOTIMES is similar to:

```
(DO ((X 0 (+ 1 X)))
    ((< X NUM) RETURN)
    (CONTENTS)
```

Use a "do" loop when a loop must exit based on the value of an evaluation within the loop. But if you only want to do something a fixed number of times, then DOTIMES should be your choice.

MAPPING

Another method of performing iteration in LISP does not require a loop. Mapping is a LISP function applied to a sequence of arguments. There are several primitives in Common LISP that are often called *maps* because they allow sequences to be mapped over by functions.

MAPCAR

Let's first discuss MAPCAR, which successively applies a function to each element in the list or lists that serve as its argument. The following example uses MAPCAR to add each individual element in one list to the corresponding element in the second list:

```
(MAPCAR #'+ '(1 2 3) '(4 5 6))
```

This expression evaluates to (5 7 9), which is the result of:

```
(+ 1 4)
(+ 2 5)
(+ 3 6)
```

MAPCAR does not limit the number of lists that can serve as arguments; therefore, the following expression is perfectly valid:

```
(MAPCAR #'+ '(1 2 3) '(4 5 6) '(7 8 9))
```

This expression evaluates to (12 15 18), which is the result of:

```
(+ 1 (+ 4 7))
(+ 2 (+ 5 8))
(+ 3 (+ 6 9))
```

Notice that MAPCAR accepts two different kinds of arguments. The first is preceded by the octothorpe (#) (also called a "hash mark," "number sign," or "pound sign") and a single quote. This sequence identifies a LISP function. It is this argument that is mapped or applied to the elements of a list. These mapped elements make up the second type of argument.

When MAPCAR runs out of elements in a list, it does not process the elements in other lists. For example:

```
(MAPCAR #'+ '(14) '(1 2 3))
```

evaluates to (15), because there is only one element in the first list. The last two elements of the second list are not applied. Likewise:

```
(MAPCAR #'+ '(1 2 3) '(14))
```

evaluates to (15), because the last argument is a single list element.

This example of MAPCAR uses the ABS math primitive:

```
(MAPCAR #'ABS '(1 -2 3 -4 5 -6 7 -8))
```

This evaluates to (1 2 3 4 5 6 7 8), which is a list of the absolute values of each of the elements in the argument list.

EVERY

EVERY is a Common LISP function that maps a predicate over an entire sequence of arguments; it returns True (T) if every sequence proves true. If a sequence is NIL, then EVERY returns NIL. Each sequence argument must be a list. The following example of EVERY tests whether the first element in each list is less than the second element:

```
(EVERY #'< '(1 2) '(2 3) '(3 4) '(5 6))
```

This results in a true return, because:

```
(< 1 2)  =  T
(< 2 3)  =  T
(< 3 4)  =  T
(< 5 6)  =  T
```

The following example returns NIL:

```
(EVERY #'= '(1 1) '(2 2) '(3 3) '(4 5))
```

NIL occurs because the last list contains two elements that are not equal. If a predicate test on a list used as an argument to EVERY proves NIL, then EVERY returns NIL.

MAPCAR cannot accomplish the same task, although a predicate argument is perfectly acceptable. For instance:

```
(MAPCAR #'< '(1 2) '(2 3) '(3 4) '(5 6))
```

returns:

```
(T T T)
```

because the use of the less than predicate proved true on the first three argument lists. The evaluation ended with the fourth argument, because it returned NIL when mapped by the less than predicate.

There are other ways of dealing with loops and iteration in Common LISP. This chapter has highlighted some of the major areas. BASIC programmers may feel most comfortable performing iteration with a "do" loop, since this is roughly similar to FOR-NEXT and WHILE-WEND loops in BASIC. However, many operations can be performed more easily and directly through the use of mapping and the functions that address this form of iteration. Another chapter in this book will show how to use the "do" loop in writing several math-related functions.

Chapter 8

LISP Conditionals

Conditionals are found in every computer language. These tools may be called conditional operators, conditional statements, conditional constructs and many other names, but they all have one thing in common: They each do something based upon the result of a simple test. This is usually a binary test, or several tests that ultimately evaluate to a binary test. In the end, this test can be boiled down to true or false, yes or no, plus or minus, or some other binary terminology.

In BASIC, the best-known conditional is the IF-THEN-ELSE statement. The IF portion performs the specified test. THEN reads the instructions that are to carried out if the test proves true. ELSE provides another set of instructions should the test prove false. For example, take the following BASIC program line:

```
100 IF X=Y THEN Z=10 ELSE Z=5
```

The specified test compares the values of the variables X and Y. If the two are equal, "true" is returned and execution switches to the THEN construct, where variable Z is assigned a value of 10. However, should the IF test prove false, execution moves to the ELSE construct, whose instruction tells the computer to assign a value of 5 to the variable Z.

IF AND IFN

LISP also contains a primitive equivalent to the IF-THEN-ELSE statement. IF evaluates the equivalent of the THEN instruction or the ELSE instruction in BASIC. It is used in the familiar format of:

(IF *test* THEN <*form*> ELSE <*form*>)

The BASIC example is written in LISP as:

```
(IF (= X Y) (SETQ Z 10) (SETQ Z 5))
```

(assuming symbols X and Y contain numeric values). Notice that there is no actual use of "then" or "else." Just remember that the first form that follows the predicate is evaluated if the test is true while the second form is evaluated if the test is false. If X is indeed equal to Y, then the SETQ primitive assigns the value 10 to the symbol Z. If X is not equal to Y, then SETQ assigns Z a value of 5 in the second form.

Here is another example:

```
(IF (< X Y) 1 2)
```

This form evaluates to 1 if X is less than Y or to Z if X is equal to or more than Y. We can also display a message on the monitor screen using the following example:

```
(IF (< X Y) 'SMALLER 'LARGER)
```

If X is less than Y, SMALLER is returned. If X is equal to or greater than Y, the form evaluates to the atom LARGER. It is not necessary to use PRINT to get this return. However, if you want a return message to include more than one word (atom), it is necessary to use an appropriate primitive in constructing the form. For example:

```
(IF (< X Y) (PRINT "X IS SMALLER")
    (PRINT "X IS LARGER")
```

The LISP conditional IFN operates in a reverse manner to IF and is called IFN (for "if-not" or "not-test"). It uses this format:

(IF (*not test*) THEN <*form*> ELSE <*form*>)

IFN works just like IF except that the first form (then) is evaluated if the test proves untrue. The else form is evaluated if the test proves true. For example:

```
(IFN (= X Y) 1 2)
```

evaluates to 1 if X is not equal to Y or to 2 if X is equal to Y. We may think of this as:

```
(IFN <not> (= X Y) 1 2)
```

or

```
(IF (NEQ X Y) 1 2)
```

or

```
(IF (NOT '(= X Y)) 1 2)
```

The last two examples are the IF equivalents of the IFN form.

Since there is little difference between the IF and IFN and forms in Common LISP and the IF-THEN-ELSE statement in BASIC, BASIC language programmers should have little difficulty with these LISP conditionals. Of course, IF and IFN limit their then-else forms to only one each. Difficulties arise when trying to duplicate a BASIC program line such as:

```
100 IF X = Y
    THEN PRINT Z:F = 1:H = 14
    ELSE PRINT D:F = 5:H = 0
```

Fortunately, LISP offers other methods to handle this, about which, we will learn more later in this chapter.

We can use IF and IFN to perform a multitude of tests and then evaluate the ELSE or the THEN form depending on the outcome. An example of a multiple test IF-THEN-ELSE line in BASIC is:

```
100 IF X=Y OR I=10 THEN R=7 ELSE R=6
```

If either X = Y or I = 10 is true then R = 7. If X is not equal to Y *and* I is not equal to 10, then the ELSE portion of this conditional is executed and R = 6. In LISP, this line appears

```
(IF (OR (= X Y) (= I 10))
    (SETQ R 7) (SETQ R 6))
```

In both examples the logical OR operator performs the tests for IF. The next example uses the logical AND operator:

```
(IF (AND (EQUAL X Y) (> I J)) 'K 'P)
```

In this test,the THEN form is evaluated only when X is equal to Y and I is more than J. The THEN form evaluates to "K" while the ELSE form evaluates to "P." Notice that the EQUAL predicate is used instead of an " = ." This example assumes that symbols X and Y represent nonnumeric values.

Logical operators allow IF tests to be as complex as needed. This makes IF and IFN extremely valuable tools for the LISP programmer.

WHEN

In Common LISP, the WHEN conditional evaluates more than one form when a test proves non-NIL. It is used in a similar fashion to IF except there is no ELSE form. Evaluation takes place only when the test proves true. The following BASIC program line is best converted to LISP using WHEN:

```
100 IF X=Y THEN T=1:R=4:S=14
```

A single test determines whether X is equal to Y. If it is, then three other variables are assigned values. In Common LISP, we can simulate this with:

```
(WHEN (= X Y) (SETQ T 1) (SETQ R 4) (SETQ S 14))
```

WHEN evaluates each form if the test result is non-NIL. Only the result of the last form is returned. This line returns 14 because the last form evaluates to this. However, since this example uses SETQ to assign symbols, the return value is unimportant. Instead, we want to assign symbols, T, R, and S numeric values. This assignment occurs when the test proves true. The return value of the final form indicates only that the test proved true. If the test proves NIL then the return value is NIL.

Don't try a multiple return with WHEN, as in:

```
(WHEN (= X Y) 'TEST 'PROVES 'TRUE)
```

This won't work. The return will be TRUE assuming that the test is non-NIL, because 'TRUE is the last of the series of forms to be evaluated.

We can use the VALUES primitive in Common LISP to obtain multiple returns:

```
(SETQ A 'TEST)
(SETQ B 'PROVES)
(SETQ C 'TRUE)
(WHEN (= X Y) (VALUES A B C))
```

This example returns:

```
TEST
PROVES
TRUE
```

90

Multiple return values are rarely needed. The preceding example is more simply written as:

```
(IF (= X Y) 'TEST-PROVES-TRUE)
```

This assumes you want a messagelike return. Remember, the return is simply the printed evaluation of the last form handed to WHEN. The other forms are also evaluated, but their evaluations are not returned to the screen. To print these other evaluations, you need to use a PRINT primitive as in:

```
(IF (= X Y)
(PRINT 'TEST) (PRINT 'PROVES) 'TRUE)
```

This gives you your message, but only the last form's evaluation is a *return*. The other screen writes occur because of the Common LISP primitive PRINT.

UNLESS

UNLESS works like THEN in reverse. UNLESS is equivalent to THEN just as IFN is equivalent to IF. Both IFN and UNLESS evaluate a form when the test proves NIL. For example:

```
(UNLESS (= X Y) (SETQ X 1) (SETQ Y 2))
```

The two forms are evaluated only when X is not equal to Y. In words, this line reads, "Assign X a value of 1 and Y a value of 2, *unless* X is equal to Y." It is the same as:

```
(WHEN (NEQ X Y) (SETQ X 1) (SETQ Y 2))
```

or

```
(WHEN (NOT (= X Y))
(SETQ X 1) (SETQ Y 2))
```

Sometimes it is easier to use UNLESS rather than WHEN for program clarity or when a multitude of tests have to be run, each of which must evaluate to NIL in order to evaluate other forms.

THE CASE CONDITIONAL

The Common LISP conditional CASE is a special form that determines matches, returning an appropriate value or message depending on whether or not a match is found. The following program demonstrates CASE:

```
(CASE (+ X Y) ((2 4 6 8) 'EVEN)
              ((1 3 5 9) 'ODD)
              (OTHERWISE ' OUT-OF-RANGE))
```

CASE first evaluates (+ X Y). Assuming that X is equal to 1 and Y is equal to 3, this form evaluates to 4. CASE then looks for a match in the clauses that follow. Each clause contains a key. In this example, the key is represented by the numbers contained in parentheses. If a match is found, CASE evaluates the next form in the clause. Here the evaluation is EVEN since the key form (+ X Y) evaluates to 4 and the clause key (2 4 6 8) contains a match. The clause form 'EVEN is therefore evaluated and returned. If X had a value of 1 and Y had a value of 2, then there would be no match and evaluation would move on to the next clause. Since the key form would then evaluate to 3, the second clause match form would be evaluated and ODD would be returned.

As a final example, suppose X and Y are both equal to zero. Since no match would be found in either of the first two clauses, the last clause is a "do if all else fails" safety valve. OTHERWISE is like ELSE in a BASIC IF-THEN-ELSE statement. Its form is evaluated and returned. Here the return would be OUT-OF-RANGE.

The use of CASE in this examples is similar to the following BASIC program logic:

```
100   IF X + Y = 2 OR X + Y = 4 OR X + Y = 6 OR X + Y = 8
      THEN PRINT "EVEN"
      ELSE IF X + Y = 1 OR X + Y = 3 OR X + Y = 5 OR X + Y = 7 OR X + Y = 9
          THEN PRINT "ODD"
          ELSE PRINT "OUT-OF-RANGE"
```

It is easy to see that CASE can save you a lot of programming time and help you avoid possible confusion by providing a ready means for determining when a match exists. This ability to compare an argument with a list of values is especially useful in LISP, where large groups of objects must be compared in order to obtaining a match.

COND

The last LISP conditional discussed in this chapter is appropriately names. COND is a general conditional form of Common LISP. It is similar to the others already discussed and more or less combines most of their attributes. However, it is slower than IF, IFN, CASE, WHEN, and UNLESS, so it should be used only when these other conditionals are inappropriate or inconvenient for program clarity.

COND allows the performance of many different tests as individual objects. Each test is accompanied by a single form that is evaluated when the test proves true. Regardless of the number of test clauses (Note: A test clause contains a test and a form to be evaluated if the test is true.), the first clause that evaluates non-NIL becomes the first clause to have it evaluated and returned. Evaluation of the test clause chain then ends.

The following example demonstrates the use of COND in Common LISP:

```
(SETQ X 14)
(COND ((= X 1) 'ONE)
      ((> X 15) (/ X 2))
      ((= X 14) (* X 2))
      (T  (VALUES X)))
```

X has the value 14. COND tests the value of X using several LISP predicates. On the first COND line, if X is equal to 1 then ONE is returned. The second line returns X / 2 when X is more than 15. The third line returns X * 2 when X is equal to 14. In this example 28 is returned, because X is indeed equal to 14. When this is detected, the matching form is evaluated, which results in 28.

The last line in this example is not evaluated because the test on the previous line proved true. However, this is a traditional last line in a COND form and it serves as the equivalent of ELSE in a BASIC IF-THEN-ELSE statement. The T, or course, is the LISP symbol meaning true. Therefore, this last line is always evaluated if all the previous tests are NIL. If this last line is omitted, then COND evaluates to NIL and returns this value, assuming that all the previous test clauses also evaluated to NIL.

The Common LISP conditionals form a very important set of tools for effectively testing the whole range of LISP evaluations. Conditionals are used in every program language. Common LISP has more than most other languages,due to the special applications for which LISP is designed. Many of these conditionals may seem like simple copies of others, albeit with slightly different formats, but as you delve deeper into Common LISP you will find that each conditional has its own place and works better than all the others, given a particular programming situation.

COND occurs in many LISP programs, but I have found it best to use IF, IFN, WHEN, and UNLESS whenever practical, because of their faster execution speed. For the LISP beginner, though, program clarity is more important, initially, than execution speed. The beginner should use those LISP tools that he or she feels most comfortable with. It's a good idea to use as many different functions, predicates, and conditionals as possible in order to gain a better understanding of how each works. You will then be in a better position to decide which serves best in programming LISP applications.

Chapter 9

Common LISP Data Types

This chapter is short and sweet. It deals with LISP data types, which can be unnecessarily confusing to beginners. In LISP, programmers are often more concerned with objects than with data types. Generally, an object is an object regardless of the data category it happens to fall into, and it's treated as an object by the function or procedure that handles it. This may be oversimplifying things a bit, but as you learn LISP you will find yourself thinking less and less of data types and more and more about what various objects name or represent.

In Common LISP a data type may be a single object, but more often it is a group of individual objects that are represented as a single entity. Therefore, data types become a bit muddy, because numbers, strings, characters, etc., may be used to construct a set that is of a particular data type, although it contains elements that, in themselves, are different data types.

NUMBERS

Common LISP offers several kinds of numbers. The actual number of subtypes depends on the LISP package you are using; the full Common LISP set includes INTEGER, RATIO, FLOAT, and COMPLEX number types. Each of these can be broken down into more subtypes.

An integer is a whole number such as 1, 2, 3, 4, 5, etc. Floating point numbers are signified by a decimal as in 1.0, 2.0, 3.0, 4.0, 5.0, etc. Floating-point numbers may have fractional components, whereas integers do not. In LISP, 4.0 and 4 are not the same number. The first is a float while the second is an integer. This is important to know when you have to compare the values of numbers. There are LISP functions that signify the equality of two numbers if they are mathematically equal to the same value, which is the case of 4.0 and 4. However, other functions may indicate equality only when two numbers are *identical*. Those functions would find 4.0 and 4 unequal.

Ratios are numbers that represent the mathematical ratio of two integers, such as 2/4, 3/4, 4/5, 8/3, etc. These are different from common division operations. But if a ratio that is evenly divisible, results between two integers, then this division is performed and the result is returned.

Complex numbers are not dealt with in this book. They are numbers represented in Cartesian form with a real part and an imaginary part. Each of these parts is a noncomplex number that may be an integer, a float, or a ratio.

Integers

An integer is a whole number. Digital computers can process integers much faster than they can process floating-point numbers, so integers are used whenever possible in computations. In Common LISP there are two basic categories of integers: *fixnum* and *bignum*. Fixnums are smaller than bignums and they are handled more efficiently by the computer. The actual range (from negative to positive) of a fixnum dependents on the computer used to implement Common LISP.

Golden Common LISP for the IBM PC has a fixnum range from -32768 to $+32767$. This is also the standard range of integer values when programming 16-bit computers, although larger integers are accepted. Integers beyond this range are sometimes known as *longs* or *long integers*. In Common LISP, these integers are called bignums. The range of bignums is again dependent on the computer used for implementation.

The Golden Common LISP Common LISP package used to research this book did not support bignums. This was not a great handicap, since larger numbers can be represented as floats. For instance, the value 42,000 lies outside the fixnum range, but 42,000.0 is a floating-point number and is perfectly legal.

When performing mathematical operations on numbers in any language, it is always best to use integers where possible. BASIC programmers may find it difficult to understand the difference between integers and floats with no fractional value. The following

FOR-NEXT loop in BASIC is highly inefficient and an example of poor programming technique:

```
10 FOR X=1 TO 2000
20 PRINT X
30 NEXT
```

Better than 75 percent of the BASIC programmers who do not make a living in the computer field will not find anything wrong with this program. I'm sure every reader, regardless of his or her present skills, has written programs using such a loop. This includes myself as well. Never again, though.

The problem with this program is its inefficiency, specifically the variable X. This is a floating-point variable. But why use a floating-point variable when all it represents is integer values, those whole numbers from 1 to 2000? BASIC lets us get away with murder when it comes to number handling. Most other languages are more demanding.

When executing this BASIC program, the computer increments each value of X as a floating-point value since X is a floating-point variable. Therefore, when X = 1, the computer sees it as X = 1.0000000. It must check through to the last decimal place before determining that there is no fractional portion to this floating-point. This takes far more time than it would if X were an integer variable. The PRINT statement must also check to the last decimal place of X for a fractional component before printing an integer representation to the monitor screen.

The program is properly written as follows:

```
10 FOR X%=1 TO 2000
20 PRINT X%
30 NEXT X%
```

This program runs much faster than the former. Variable X% is an integer variable indicated by the trailing % and the computer is not be hog-tied while searching for fractions that don't exist.

This is not a book on programming in BASIC, but its reader will undoubtedly include many BASIC programmers who are exploring a language other than BASIC for the first time. Common LISP does not have a special way of designating variables to hold different types of numbers as BASIC does (% for integer; # for double-precision floating point, etc.), so you must be aware of the types of numbers you assign to variables. The BASIC IF-THEN test:

```
IF 4 = 4.0 THEN do something
```

will prove true, but Common LISP may find the two numbers totally different entities, depending on the type of predicate used to make the test. You need to know just what constitutes an integer, a bignum, a fixnum, a float, etc., handle mathematics efficiently in Common LISP.

Note: LISP is known as a nonmathematical language. Don't believe it! While LISP is more concerned with the manipulation of data objects, mathematics does play a large role. This is evidenced by the number of expensive LISP auxiliary math packages, available. These are aimed at the owners of older LISP programming packages that were all but devoid of the usual math functions.

Floats

Floating-point numbers have a fractional component. These numbers may have an integer component as well e.g., 4.6687. The 4 is the integer component while 0.6687 is the fractional component. Others may contain only a fractional component. In 0.7692, for example, the integer component is missing from a practical point of view, although 0 is an integer in the truest sense of the word.

In Common LISP, all floating-point numbers are called *floats*. However, floats may have subcategories, depending on their values and the Common LISP program being used. These subcategories include *short-float, single-float, double-float,* and *long-float*. Most LISP implementations combine short- and single-floats as well as double- and long-floats into two subcategories. The value range of each category depends on the LISP package implementation and the computer used.

With Golden Common LISP on the IBM Personal Computer, floating-point values can range from 1.0F − 38 to 6.80565F + 38, positive or negative. Other implementations will probably have different floating-point ranges. Single-precision floating-point values are expressed in standard decimal format as in 4.5, 1.0, 0.0. Double-precision floats are expressed in what is called scientific notation: 4.5DO, 1.0DO, 0.0DO. These numbers are the double-precision equivalents of the first set of single-precision floating-point numbers.

CHARACTERS AND STRINGS

Common LISP character data types include letters in various styles and, possibly, different alphabets. Character data types are normally broken down into two subcategories: *standard-char* and *string-char*.

Standard-char is equivalent to the standard ASCII character set embedded in your microcomputer. It is composed of 95 characters, including the upper-and lowercase standard alphabet, certain punctuation marks and symbols, etc.

String-char characters are those that can appear in strings or printable characters. Standard-char is a subcategory of string-char.

Put simply, *strings* in Common LISP are composed of characters enclosed by double quotes. For example:

"HELLO"

is a string while:

'HELLO

is a name or symbol. When strings are printed or returned by LISP functions, the surrounding double quotes are also returned; these identify the object as a string and are part of its makeup.

LISTS

A list is the basic data structure of LISP. Lists are collections of objects bound together as a single object. Lists have subtypes, one of which is CONS. CONS is a data structure composed of two alterable components traditionally called the CAR and the CDR. Common LISP redefines these terms as FIRST and REST. A CONS usually represents lists but this is not always true, because of CONS can also represent a dotted pair list, which is not a true list. A detailed explanation of lists and CONS is presented in another chapter.

This discussion on data types is merely rough overview. In LISP, we need not be terribly concerned about data types, at least not at the beginning. LISP programmers are mainly concerned about objects, which can comprise any and all data types. Operations are performed on objects without much regard to their data types.

In LISP we are primarily concerned with *lists* and *atoms* as objects. The next chapter discusses this subject more thoroughly. Lists can be thought of as objects that contain removable or alterable data. Atoms are objects that are not alterable. Single letters, words, and numbers are atoms. Collections of atoms can form lists, as can collections of other lists.

Since there are only two primary types of objects in LISP, a full discussion of LISP's many different or discrete data types is unreasonable at this time. LISP is not a difficult language to learn, but it does require a little rethinking of rid yourself of prejudices built up from programming in BASIC or other languages.

Chapter 10

Fun with Functions

This chapter will discuss the building of personal LISP functions. These functions are the miniprograms you build from other Common LISP functions to address your personal programming needs.

In LISP, we are not stuck with LISP's built-in set of primitives. Unlike BASIC, we can add functions to our standard Common LISP library. This means that often repeated procedures do not have to be reprogrammed every time they are used but can be constructed, saved, and called just like any other LISP function.

To keep things simple, we will use functions that have been previously discussed to build new functions. Some of these personal functions may copy or closely mimic standard LISP functions, but this is only because the massive Common LISP function set has been constructed from very common primitives.

VARIATIONS ON FIRST AND REST

Let's begin by building some simple functions to access different elements of a list. Assume that the only primitives we have for this job are FIRST and REST.

ASSIGNMENT: Write a procedure for finding the second element in a list.

The correct combination of FIRST and REST gives us:

```
(FIRST (REST LISTARG))
```

In this example, LISTARG is a variable assigned the value of the list from which the second element is to be returned. If LISTARG is equal to:

```
(A B C D E)
```

then:

```
(REST '(A B C D E))  =  (B C D E)
```

and

```
(FIRST '(B C D E))  =  B
```

This combination therefore gives us a procedure that returns the second element of this list argument.

To make this procedure a usable Common LISP function we write:

```
(DEFUN SECOND (ARG)
 (FIRST (REST ARG)))
```

DUFUN is used by first naming the new function (SECOND), and then giving its argument(s) symbol(s) in parentheses. This argument is used with the LISP primitive FIRST and REST to make SECOND do what we want.

Now that we have built the function using DEFUN, we can use SECOND like any other LISP function. For example:

```
(SECOND '(1 2 3 4))
```

This returns the second element in the list: 2.

Nearly every Common LISP programming package contains a SECOND function as well as a THIRD and so on. But suppose we want to enhance the built-in function so that it allows two lists to serve as arguments, the second element of each list being returned as a list with two element, as in:

```
(SECOND2 '(A B C) '(D E F))  =  (B E)
```

The new function, named SECOND2, takes the second element from the first list argument and the second element from the second list argument, and combines the two in a new list. It can be written as:

```
(DEFUN SECOND2 (ARG1 ARG2)
 (LIST (FIRST (REST ARG1))
        (FIRST (REST ARG2))))
```

The progression of this function is:

```
(FIRST (REST '(A B C))) =  'B
(FIRST (REST '(D E F))) =  'E
(LIST 'B 'E)            =  (B E)
```

This function returns a list composed of the second element of the first list argument and the second element of the last list argument.

Since we already have a SECOND function that actually performs this procedure:

```
(FIRST (REST ARG))
```

SECOND2 can be written more simply with the following:

```
(DEFUN SECOND2 (ARG1 ARG2)
  (LIST (SECOND ARG1) (SECOND ARG2)))
```

Either procedure gives the same results.

Writing LISP functions is excellent practice and it's fun. Undoubtedly, your first efforts will generate many error messages and your first successful functions may not be as efficient as they could be. Still, writing functions allows you to practice and hone your skills on small applications that are logical and practical.

When writing a function that accepts more than one argument, notice how the arguments are represented. All arguments are enclosed in a single set of parentheses. Some beginning programmers tend to express this as:

```
(DEFUN FUNCTION (ARG1) (ARG2)
```

This is incorrect; it will yield an error message every time the function is called.

We can further modify SECOND2 to combine the second elements in three list arguments with this procedure:

```
(DEFUN SECOND2 (ARG1 ARG2 ARG3)
  (LIST (SECOND ARG1)
        (SECOND ARG2)
        (SECOND ARG3)))
```

A slight rewrite of the original version of SECOND yields a function that returns a list comprised of the second element from the last argument and the second element of the first argument. The return is a list that reverses the elements. This function can be written as:

```
(DEFUN SECOND2 (ARG1 ARG2)
  (LIST (SECOND ARG2) (SECOND ARG1)))
```

Variations of this are almost limitless.

FIRST-LAST

The following discussion builds another personalized function.

ASSIGNMENT: Build a function that returns a list composed of the first and last elements of the argument list.

We can easily construct such a function using FIRST, REST, LAST, and LIST in a procedure similar to this one:

```
(LIST (FIRST ARG) (FIRST (LAST ARG)))
```

Let's break this procedure down using ' (A B C D E F) as the argument.

```
1.  (LAST '(A B C D E F))     =   (F)
2.  (FIRST '(F))              =   'F
3.  (FIRST '(A B C D E F)     =   'A
4.  (LIST 'A 'B)              =   (A B)
```

The final result is what we are looking for. The function can be written as:

```
(DEFUN FIRST-LAST (ARG)
  (LIST (FIRST ARG) (FIRST (LAST ARG))))
```

Now we can use:

```
(FIRST-LAST '(A B C D E F))
```

to return the list:

```
(A F)
```

A and F are the first and last elements of the list argument.

Watch out for LAST. It can be confusing at first, because it doesn't work like FIRST. LAST behaves more like REST because LAST's return is a list containing the last element in the argument list. If this element is a list, then LAST returns embedded list. Think of LAST as a function that returns the argument list stripped of all but the last element.

The preceding method is perfectly satisfactory for writing FIRST-LAST, but there are many other ways of creating the same function. For example:

```
(DEFUN FIRST-LAST (ARG)
  (LIST (NTH 0 ARG)
        (NTH (- (LENGTH ARG) 1) ARG)))
```

This function does exactly the same thing as the first example, but it does not use FIRST and LAST. Rather, NTH is used to extract the first list element. The procedure:

```
(NTH 0 ARG)
```

is the same as:

```
(FIRST ARG)
```

To gain access to the last element in the argument list, LENGTH determines the total number of elements in the list. This value is reduced by one because NTH begins counting at zero. The outcome of this mathematical operation serves as the position argument for NTH, and the first element of the argument list is returned. This is the element itself and not, as would be the case with LAST, a list containing only this element.

EVERY-OTHER

The following assignment makes things a bit more complex.

ASSIGNMENT: Write a function that returns a list whose elements are every other element of the argument list.

The function EVERY-OTHER is a variation of FIRST-LAST and is a bit more complex to program. The purpose of this function is to return a list that contains every other element of the argument list. The returned list will contain elements that match the first, third, fifth, etc., elements of the argument list. For example:

```
(EVERY-OTHER '(A B C D E F G))   =   (A C E G)
```

This function is written using a "do" loop to read through the elements of the argument list. FIRST and REST extract the first element of the REST of the argument list. Each loop pass reassigns the REST value to the internal value of the original argument. This does not reassign the actual argument; its value changes are common only to the function.

The procedure for EVERY-OTHER follows:

```
(DEFUN EVERY-OTHER (ARG)
  (DO ((X (LIST (FIRST ARG))
          (APPEND X (LIST (FIRST ARG)))))
      ((EQUAL (REST (REST ARG)) NIL) X)
      (SETF ARG (REST (REST ARG)))))
```

The do loop cycles until (REST (REST ARG)) equals NIL. This means that no elements remain in the list that can be accessed on

LOOP PASS NUMBER	VALUE ARG	VALUE X
1	(A B C D E F G)	(A)
2	(C D E F G)	(A C)
3	(E F G)	(A C E)
4	(G)	(A C E G)
5	( )	(A C E G) return

Fig. 10-1. Demonstration of the EVERY__OTHER function, which extracts alternate elements of a list passed to it as an argument. In this case the expression is (EVERY__OTHER ' (A B C D E F G)).

an every other element basis. Remember that the REST of a list is the original list minus its first element. Therefore, the REST of the REST of a list is the original list minus its first two elements.

SETF reassigns ARG to a value that is equal to its former list minus the first two items using REST of REST. The exit clause proves true when REST of the REST of ARG is NIL. The loop and function are exited with the return value represented by X.

When the loop is first entered, X is bound to the value of a list that contains only the FIRST of the argument list. On each loop pass, X is incremented by adding another item to its list through the use of APPEND. Remember, the internal or functional value of ARG changes on each loop pass, so the FIRST of the newly updated value of ARG will always be the equivalent of every other element in the original loop argument.

Figure 10-1 shows a typical sequence for (EVERY-OTHER ' (A B C D E F G)). The following function is exactly like the one above, except the SETF line is made a part of the exit clause (this conserves some line space):

```
(DEFUN EVERY-OTHER (ARG)
  (DO ((X (LIST (FIRST ARG))
          (APPEND X (LIST (FIRST ARG))))))
      ((EQUAL (SETF ARG (REST (REST ARG))) NIL) X)))
```

This is far more difficult to understand than the previous example, which placed each of its major operations in easily defined blocks. The exit clause compares (SETF ARG . . . .) to see if NIL was returned. This may seem unworkable to beginners, but if you SETF ARG to a NIL value, the special form will return NIL. This return is compared against NIL and if true, the loop exits with a return value of X.

REV

This next function works just like one already found in Common LISP, but REV is a good study in building LISP functions.

106

ASSIGNMENT: Write a function that will return a list whose elements are in reverse order to its argument.

Common LISP already offers REVERSE, which can do the assignment, but how is it written? In a manner similar to this function:

```
(DEFUN REV (ARG)
  (SETF A '())
  (DO ((X (- (LENGTH ARG) 1) (- X 1)))
      (((< X 0) A)
       (SETF A
         (APPEND A (LIST (NTH X ARG)))))))
```

A represents a NULL list. Within the loop it is reassigned the value of itself and each element of the argument (within a list) in reverse order. NTH's position argument is the loop variable.

Loop variable X is initially assigned a value that is the length of the argument minus 1. On each pass of the loop, this value names the element position for NTH. APPEND returns the original list contained in A with the new element appended. On the next pass of the loop, is incremented by 1, so the element positions are returned in reverse order (from right to left) and appended to A in a left-to-right order. Figure 10-2 shows the progression of this function:

```
(REV '(A B C D E F G))
```

This function simply reads items from the argument list and assigns them to another list in reverse order.

In this case, the argument list is read from right to left, but it could also read the argument elements in standard left-to-right order and write them to the new list in reverse. The following revision of the function does just that:

PASS NUMBER	VALUE A	VALUE X
1	(G)	6
2	(G F)	5
3	(G F E)	4
4	(G F E D)	3
5	(G F E D C)	2
6	(G F E D C B)	1
7	(G F E D C B A)	0

Fig. 10-2. The user-defined REV function creates a reverse-order list containing the elements of a list passed to it as an argument.

107

```
(DEFUN REV (ARG)
  (SETF A '())
  (DO ((X O (+ 1 X)))
      ((= (LENGTH ARG)) A)
      (SETF A
      (APPEND (LIST (NTH X ARG)) A))))
```

As we wanted, this function reads the argument list from left to
right and returns the new list arguments from right to left. As each
new element is read from ARG, it is placed in front of (to the left)
of the element that was previously placed in the return list. Loop
variable X is counted from 0 to (LENGTH ARG) minus 1.

In the previous REV function, the reverse list sequence was
from left to right as in:

```
(G  F  E ......)
```

but the revised version of REV builds the list in reverse:

```
(.......C  B  A)
```

The end result is the same, but the methods used to construct the
two reverse lists are different. The first method appends elements,
read from the argument in right-to-left order, to the new list in left-
to-right order. The second function reads elements from left to
right, appending the old list to the new list containing a single list
element.

Another way to use the left-to-right reading of the argument
list and the right-to-left writing of the return list is through the list
of CONS. As you remember, if the second argument to CONS is
a list, then you can think of the first argument object as being added
to the front of the list. Therefore, we can read:

```
A  B  C  D ......
```

and write each character to another list as:

```
...... D  C  B  A
```

The following function uses CONS to construct the reversed
list. It is not necessary to use LIST, because CONS can use another data object for its first argument and add it to the front of
the list that serves as its second argument:

```
(DEFUN REV (ARG)
  (SETF A '())
  (DO ((X O (+ 1 X)))
      ((= X (LENGTH ARG)) A)
      (SETF A (CONS (NTH X ARG) A))))
```

There are many other ways to write this same function. The three methods shown produce efficient, workable functions and each method is instructive.

CUSTOM MATHEMATICAL FUNCTIONS

The view that LISP is not a mathematical language and doesn't need complex math functions is part of the past, we hope. However, there are still a fair number of LISP development packages which do not provide an acceptable set of math functions. These include a function to return the square root of a number; a function to return the log of a number; and EXP functions; and SIN and COS functions.

Even the first versions of Golden Common LISP did not have these functions (current versions do). While many LISP applications do not require complex math functions, this does not apply to all LISP applications. One is never at a loss when these math functions are provided and the time is bound to come when they are necessary for a particular application.

I am accustomed to "doing without" these functions, because I have used many "just released" programming packages in several different languages. Traditionally, the first versions of these are capable of performing basic arithmetic operations like add, subtract, multiply, and divide, but nothing more complex is provided. If such functions are needed, they must be either written by the user or purchased as an adjunct software package. These adjuncts can cost nearly as much as the "pioneer version" development packages.

A few years ago I tired of waiting for software developers to update their compilers and interpreters to include the most-needed math functions and decided to learn how to write my own. I experimented for many months and gave up several times. Even a mundane complex function like square root is extremely difficult to program unless you have a high-level math background or a good reference work on mathematics.

I finally found the latter. It was pure Greek at first, but I struggled through the formulas, most of which contained symbols that I had never seen before. In the end I was able to write a full set of math functions, quite a few of which were faster and more accurate than those offered in expensive adjunct software.

In this section we will explore a few of the complex math functions. If you're using a current version of Golden Common LISP, these won't be necessary, but they may be educational. If you have a LISP interpreter or compiler that does not have these functions, you can put them to practical advantage as well.

SQRT

No matter what language you program in, a square root function is mandatory. The following function uses a Newtonian Approximation to derive the square root of a number. Precision should be good with most argument values to 10 to 12 decimal places. This approximation was obtained from a mathematical formula reference book and input in prefix notation:

```
(DEFUN SQRT (ARG)
  (SETF ARG (ABS ARG))
  (DO ((Y (/ ARG 2.0D0 (SETF Y
          (/ (+ Y (/ ARG Y)) 2.0D0)))))
      ((< (ABS (- (* Y Y) ARG)) 1.0D-10) Y)))
```

This is a fairly short function, but it is quite powerful, very accurate, and fast. The Newton formula it is derived from is:

$$SQRT = ((ARG1/(APPROX) + (APPROX)) / 2$$

This formula outputs the square root of ARG with very high accuracy, providing that the value of APPROX closely approximates the square root of ARG. However, the computer can't "know" that an approximation of the square root of 5 is " 2 something, " so we make a rough approximation of the square root of ARG as (ARG/2).

The output from this formula is not a good approximation of the square root of ARG—at least not the first time. However, the first output from this formula is a closer approximation of the square root of ARG than was (ARG/2), so we simply feed the first output back into the formula, substituting this for APPROX. Each new output is fed back into the formula. The VALUE of ARG never changes because it is the number from which we want the square root. It is the value of APPROX that is changed each time the formula runs. After several passes through the formula the output no longer changes. In other words, APPROX is equal to the square root of ARG.

The exit clause in the function checks that the value of Y (the square root return variable) times Y is less than .0000000001 1.0D-10 of ARG. In other words, if the square root approximation squared is within a "hair" of ARG or equal to it, then the do loop that runs APPROX is exited with a return value of Y.

As an additional feature, SETF makes certain that the ARG's value is positive. A negative value does not have a real square root because a negative number multiplied by itself always results in a positive value. Thus, a true square root is always a positive value. Should SQRT be handed a negative ARG value, it is reassigned the *absolute value* of the argument using ABS. ABS is unnecessary if you are certain the function will always be used with positive arguments, but using the absolute value of ARG is a nice safety feature that adds quality to such a function.

Note that we have used what is often called scientific notation. Instead of writing:

```
(/ B 2)
```

The scientific notation is:

```
(/ B 2.0D0)
```

The notation says to divide B by the double floating-point value of 2.0. This alerts the computer to handle the mathematics in double floating-point format, so we get a 14-place return instead of a six-place return, which would be the case with the single floating point format. If this notation is not used, the return values from this function would be in single floating-point form.

You can compare this function against any commercial version for microcomputers and find that it is just as accurate, if not more so. It may even be as fast.

4TH-ROOT

The Newtonian Approximation is applicable not only to square root approximations, but to approximations in general. It is mainly useful for taking integer roots of numbers or roots 1, 2, 3, 4, 5, 6, etc. However, with SQRT we can return an even-numbered root through *recursion*.

Put simply, recursion is a function calling itself. One might think that a pyramiding effect would thus take place, but it does not, providing a function calls itself according to a conditional test and does not call itself when the test is NIL.

For a simple excursion into recursion, let's use the previously build SQRT function to return the fourth root of a number:

```
(SQRT (SQRT 16))
```

This is the same as taking the fourth root of 16, which is 2. The progression is:

```
1. (SQRT 16)    =    4
2. (SQRT 4)     =    2
```

We have used recursion before in examples like:

```
(REST (REST '(A B C D)))
```

where REST ' (A B C D) is (B C D) and REST ' (B C D) is CD.

111

We can also obtain the sixth root of a number with:

```
(SQRT (SQRT (SQRT 256)))
```

The progression is:

```
1.  (SQRT 256)    =       16
2.  (SQRT 16)     =        4
3.  (SQRT 4)      =        2
```

With SQRT, you can derive roots, 2, 4, 8, 16, 32, etc.

A function called 4TH-RT can be constructed easily to return the fourth root of its argument with the following procedure:

```
(DEFUN 4TH-RT (ARG)
 (SQRT (SQRT ARG)))
```

That's all there is to it, but let's go a step further and write 2-OR-4-RT, which returns either the square or fourth root, depending on the value of the second argument. This function uses the same sequence followed in writing SQRT and calls itself once if the fourth root is specified. It is an excellent demonstration of LISP recursion:

```
(DEFUN 2-OR-4-RT (ARG RT)
 (SETF ARG (ABS ARG))
 (DO ((Y (/ ARG 2.0D0) (SETF Y (/ ARG Y)) 2.0D0))))
     ((< (ABS (- (* Y Y) ARG)) 1.0D-10)
     (IF (= RT 4) (2-OR-4-RT Y 2) Y))))
```

This function is exactly like the previously constructed SQRT, but with one exception. IF is part of the exit clause and determines the exit value. If RT (the second argument to this function) equals to 4, then the exit return is:

```
(2-OR-4-RT Y 2)
```

Remember, at this point Y represents the square root of ARG. Thus this function is called again. This time the value of 2 is used for RT, signifying the desire for a square root return. Through recursion, the square root of ARG is passed once more through the same function. During this second stage, the IF test finds that RT is now equal to 2, so the THEN portion of this special form returns the value of Y. This symbol is now equal to the square root of the square root of ARG; that is, it is the fourth root of ARG.

This function can return either the square or fourth root of ARG, depending which is specified in the second argument to this function.

It is easier to build SQRT and use DEFUN to define 4TH-

ROOT as (SQRT (SQRT ARG)), but this example effectively teaches one use of recursion.

CUBRT

As we have already stated, the Newtonian Approximation can conveniently take any integer root of a number. This approximation is used below in writing CUBRT, a function that returns the cube root of its argument:

```
(DEFUN CUBRT (ARG)
 (DO ((Y (/ X 3.0D0)
 (SETF Y (/ (+ (/ ARG (* Y Y))
 (* 2.0D0 Y)) 3.0D0))))
 ((< (ABS (- (* Y Y Y) ARG)) 1.0D-10) Y)))
```

CUBRT uses the Newtonian formula as follows:

```
CUBRT = ((ARG/(ARG/3) + 2*(ARG/3)) / 3
```

In the function, the symbol Y represents ARG/3; the numeric constants are specified in double floating-point format. Like the SQRT function, ARG/3 is a rough approximation that is only used for the formula during the first pass of the "do" loop. Thereafter, the output from this formula replaces ARG/3 and is represented by Y.

The exit clause is similar to the one used for SQRT, but here Y's value is cubed (* Y Y Y); this result is tested against the value of the original argument (ARG).

The accuracy of this function is excellent and compares well with most commercial versions of CUBRT. This version however, is quite slow when run under an interpreter, so a compiled version is preferred.

Notice that ARG is not processed through ABS. This is neither necessary nor desirable, since cube roots can be either positive or negative. If ARG is negative then its cube root is also be negative. Positive cube roots result from positive arguments.

Since ABS has been used in several of these functions, we should show how it is written. Remember, ABS always returns a positive value. Its main purpose is to convert negative values to positive. Positive arguments are returned unchanged. The following procedure is one way to write ABS:

```
(DEFUN ABS (ARG)
 (IF (< ARG 0) (* -1 ARG) ARG))
```

This procedure is simple. IF determines the value of ARG. If it is less than zero, then ARG is a negative number and:

```
(* -1 ARG)
```

is returned. This converts a negative value into its positive or ABS equivalent. If ARG is more than zero, then the original value of ARG is returned.

RAISE

RAISE is used to raise any root to an integer power. Again, the power must be an integer such as 2, 3, 4, 5, 6. This function takes advantage of DOTIMES and also introduces a new mathematical function:

```
(DEFUN RAISE (ROOT POW)
  (SETF Y 1.0D0)
  (COERCE ROOT 'LONG-FLOAT)
  (DOTIMES (X POW Y)
           (SETF Y (* ROOT Y))))
```

This function simply takes the root argument and multiplies it by itself for 1 less than the power (POW) value. Variable Y is initially set to 1.0D0, so on the first loop pass ROOT is multiplied by 1. On the next pass, ROOT is multiplied by ROOT. This process continues until the proper number of passes are made. When the loop exits, Y is equal to ROOT to the power POW.

The new function introduced here is COERCE. In this example, COERCE behaves much like the CDBL function in BASIC. COERCE converts the value in ROOT to a long-float. Y is initially assigned a long-float value, but ROOT is an argument whose value is unknown until the function is called. We could have accomplished the same thing with:

```
(* ROOT 1.0D0)
```

but COERCE in Common LISP handles situations such as converting one precision to another. Now of the argument, regardless of its precision, is processed in LONG-FLOAT precision.

SUMMARY

If you really want to learn Common LISP, practice buiding as many functions as you can think of. That's the nice thing about a function: it lets you use your imagination. How about a function that would return the square root of two numbers added together? Or one that will tell whether to loop continuously until a certain command is issued at the keyboard?

Functions don't have to be practical. Some of the best education possible comes from functions that do ridiculous things. Admittedly, writing functions is a bit of a novelty if you have only programmed in BASIC. Very primitive function-building capabilities are available in BASIC using DEF FN, but Common LISP gives you greater versatility.

Once you are more comfortable with Common LISP, you will be in an excellent position to start building highly useful functions that you can use over and over again to address your own programming interests.

Chapter 11

More About GLISP

Golden Common LISP from Gold Hill Computers was the model programming package used for this book. As of this writing, few Common LISP language implementations are available for personal computers, but this is changing.

The fact that Common LISP finally establishes what is hoped to be a universal LISP standard is an excellent sign for LISP. With Common LISP, the language should stabilize and other companies should soon be offering this version or updating current versions of LISP to Common LISP.

My experience with the GLISP package has been pleasant and rewarding. It is a good implementation that provides the necessary training for the beginner as well as the power for writing commercial grade applications. This broad range allows the beginner to process in Common LISP without quickly outgrowing it.

GOLD HILL SUPPORT SERVICES

Gold Hill Computers supplies customers with their Gold Hill Newsletter, which provides useful insights into their current products, policies, and future plans. Golden Common LISP is now the leading artificial intelligence language for the IBM PC. This is largely due to the extensive beta-test cycle the package went through before it was released. Gold Hill is an easy company to work with, providing excellent technical assistance and constantly upgrading their products.

While writing this book, I called Gold Hill's assistance number several times. If someone was not available immediately, I received a return call on the same day. I have heard the same glowing reports from other buyers of GCLISP.

On July 15, 1985 Carl Wolf became president and chief executive officer of Gold Hill Computers. The former president of Interactive Data Corporation is a graduate of the Harvard Business School and will certainly be using all of is abilities to keep Gold Hill on top of the AI community. One can expect Gold Hill to become even more "bullish" in this end of the market.

Being a Golden Common LISP user is almost like belonging to a club. Gold Hill Computers encourages the use of and contributes information to the Common LISP Users' Group, which is currently headed by Jerry Murray. This group (CLUG for short) is independent from Gold Hill and has three primary functions:

- To provide a Remote Bulletin Board System (RBBS).
- To build a public domain Common LISP software library.
- To provide a technical forum for Common LISP users.

This is a brand-new group, but I have accessed their bulletin board on several occasions. The offerings were a bit sparse at the start-up time, but by the time you read this it should be packed with information. The bulletin board is apparently open to anyone with an interest in Common LISP and operates at 300 or 1200 baud; it can be accessed at 617-492-2399. You can upload and download programs, leave and receive messages, take part in forums, generally wander around the system.

THE GLISP COMPILER

The GCLISP implementation used to research this book was version 1.01, which, is an interpreter. The GCLISP compiler is only now available. I have not used the compiler, but I understand that it also requires the interpreter, so you can test programs under the interpreter, and compile them for execution efficiency. Rumor has it that the compiler retails for the same price as the interpreter, $495.

Also available is GCLISP LM, which is the only MS-DOS language that can take advantage of the IBM PC-AT's full memory addressability of 16 megabytes. The LM stands for "large memory," it will be a welcome addition to PC-AT owners, who have very powerful machines and almost no software that can take advantage of this power. Most current PC-AT software is merely altered (or unaltered) standard PC software. This is like keeping your Ferrari in first gear. GCLISP LM should be a powerful artificial intelligence development tool in a machine that is well suited for the AI field.

The GCLISP compiler and GCLISP LM are in what Gold Hill calls a "gamma release" stage. This means that Gold Hill Computers thinks it has the package finished and ready for the market, but that it wants to be absolutely sure, before releasing it commercially. The gamma stage involves making the product available to a limited number of customers who agree to test the package (after signing a nondisclosure agreement) and supply feedback to the company. Gold Hill Computers will note these comments and make changes based upon outside tests. This is like a beta test being performed on the beta test. Gold Hill probably has other products undergoing gamma testing right now. This extra step for quality assurance can be quite comforting if you're planning on making a purchase.

GCLISP ENVIRONMENT INQUIRES

GCLISP offers several environment inquiry functions that are exclusive to GCLISP. These functions provide information about the implementation or perform special operations based upon the type of machine (IBM PC) GCLISP runs on.

GET-DECODED-TIME. To get a readout of system time and date, use the GET-DECODED-TIME function. It returns a *decoded* display of date and time and is used without arguments.

(GET-DECODED-TIME)

This returns the time and date units in a vertical format:

```
SECONDS
MINUTES
HOURS
DAY
MONTH
YEAR
```

For example:

```
14
28
10
16
8
1986
```

Which translates to 10:28:14 on 8/16/1986. The time zone and name of the day are not provided as they are in DOS.

You can retrieve the DOS date and time by using another GCLISP function called DOS. DOS allows for temporary exits from GCLISP into the MS-DOS environment. Using the function without an argument does not automatically return you to GCLISP once a DOS procedure is completed. To return to GCLISP typing:

```
EXIT <CR>
```

while still in the DOS environment. DOS can be used with an argument like this:

```
(DOS "DIR")
```

This brings about an exit from GCLISP to DOS where the DIR command is given. After the DOS directory is displayed, you immediately reenter the GCLISP environment.

Using DOS, we can exit to all operating system functions and run programs. Suppose we want to run a LISP program that calls a DOS program called TEST.EXE. This can be done by inserting the following line in the LISP program at the point where the MS-DOS program is to be run:

```
(DOS "TEST")
```

When GCLISP encounters this line, it exits to MS-DOS and runs TEST. When TEST has completed its run, GCLISP is reentered and the remainder of the LISP program is executed.

Warning: GCLISP requires 512K of RAM and it uses most of this in maintaining the LISP environment. MS-DOS programs to be executed after temporarily leaving GCLISP will require more memory in order to load and run. If your computer has only the minimum of 512K, then there is a good chance there won't be enough to load the DOS application. Resident system functions will be implemented without problem, but if you want to run even the smaller nonresident MS-DOS programs, then you will probably have to install more memory. With 640K you will have about 180K of memory that has not been taken up by GCLISP.

Crashes will occur if you ignore this rule. So, if you're unsure about the memory requirements of a DOS application, save your LISP program before attempting to run it, this assumes that it exits to DOS, runs a DOS application, and returns to GCLISP. If you do not do this that old "PARITY CHECK" prompt at the top left of the monitor screen might read, "I JUST ATE YOUR LISP APPLICATION."

LISP-IMPLEMENTATION-TYPE This function is used

without arguments and simply tells you what LISP implementation you are using. It is a superfluous function at present. All it returns is the string:

```
(GOLDEN Common Lisp)
```

but as GCLISP continues to grow with the GCLIP compiler, GCLISP LM, and others, this function may be helpful in determining which module of GCLISP is being used for a particular application. Those who write commercial Common Lisp applications, could use this function to provide compatibility between applications. For example, a commercial program could be made compatible with GCLISP and GCLISP LM by using LISP-IMPLEMENTATION-TYPE to determine which version to run the application. Different branches would occur, depending on what this function returns. One branch would access programs written especially for GCLISP and another would access the same programs written, for GCLISP LM.

LISP-IMPLEMENTATION-VERSION. The same use and future uses that apply to LISP-IMPLEMENTATION-TYPE also apply this function. LISP-IMPLEMENTATION-VERSION simply returns the version of GCLISP that you are using. My version is number 1.01, so this function returns the string:

```
"1.01"
```

As Gold Hill Computers comes out with improved versions of GCLISP, this function may be useful in assuring the compatibility of new LISP programs. This will be done by writing slightly different blocks of code for each version of GCLISP in areas where the two versions may be incompatible. Again, branches would occur, depending on which version is returned by this function.

FEATURES. This is a LISP variable that is reserved for LISP. This is indicated by the leading and trailing asterisks. This variable is typed in as shown with no surrounding parentheses. It is permanently assigned the value of an internally stored constant. In GCLISP version 1.01 this variable only returns GCLISP, but when the compiler is added it should also return a message indicating the compiler's presence.

Like most popular programming language software, optional features will be provided. When added to the basic interpreter, *FEATURES* will reflect their presence.

SUMMARY

GCLISPS's features are so numerous that it would require all the pages in this book to describe them in detail. This would leave no room for explaining the basics of Common LISP. GCLISP is easy to use, very powerful and very friendly. However, its range of features means that the beginner will probably takes months (not weeks) to discover all of the extra features built into it.

Beginners will be able to start programming immediately, but GCLISP contains so many extra features for debugging, editing, interacting with MS-DOS, etc., that it will take time for them to explore all the tools at their immediate disposal. This should be an exciting exploration. It is almost like Christmastime, when you know you have lots of presents and can't wait to dig in and discover what they contain!

Chapter 12

HALO Graphics

Just as this book was completed, Gold Hill Computers announced the addition of graphics capabilities to Golden Common LISP. LISP has traditionally been nongraphics language, but today graphics play a very important role in all types of computer programming. Providing at least a primitive graphics capability with nearly all programming languages is now necessary in order to allow for future expansion and to address changing applications needs.

Gold Hill Computers has not provided low-level graphics capabilities, but rather a superb, high-powered graphics standard for all microcomputers. The language is called HALO Graphics and it provides a set of powerful graphics tools in an easy-to-use graphics language.

HALO Graphics is a masterpiece of Jan Gombert of Softwriters Inc., in Baltimore, Maryland. This product is owned by Media Cybernetics Inc. of Takoma Park, Maryland which distributes it to many different software companies. Both companies have provided many (otherwise graphics-free) languages include C, FORTRAN, PASCAL, and COBOL, as well as the BASIC compiler and BASIC interpreter. Now Golden Common LISP has been added to this list.

Halo Graphics is not written in LISP. Rather, the routines are written in 8086 Assembler and called from the GCLISP environment. These routines are compiled so they run far faster than any equivalent programs would under a LISP interpreter.

Halo Graphics, then, is a set of extremely fast graphics routines, accessible from a variety of high-level languages of which Common LISP is the most recent addition. While designed primarily for the 8088/8086 MS-DOS machines, Halo Graphics is available in versions that address several different graphics device drivers, including those from IBM, *Adapter*, Tecmar, and Hercules, as well as more than a dozen others. So, regardless of the type of color board you have in your computer, there is probably a HALO Graphics package that will drive it.

THE LANGUAGE OF HALO

Halo consists of a large number of graphics primitives that act like LISP functions when called from GCLISP. HALO is actually a language itself, and the HALO functions that produce a screen display in Pascal, for example, will be the same functions used to write the same display in LISP. The only difference is how the HALO routines are called from the two languages.

There are separate HALO functions that call up or initialize the various cursors available in HALO. These include the graphics cursor (not visible on the screen); the text cursor, which displays text in different sizes, styles, and formats; and various crosshair cursors, which allow the precise placement of text and graphics images on the screen.

Other functions position the cursor at specified screen coordinates. Standard X and Y screen coordinates are used, so BASIC programmers should have little difficulty moving from IBM BASICA's graphics set to that contained in HALO graphics.

Other functions can actually write to the screen. Some are very primitive and write a single pixel on each call. Others are quite complex and draw circles, boxes triangles, lines, etc.

HALO provides functions that allow text fonts to be established and to display text in specified heights, widths, colors, and formats. Text display format can include the standard left-to-right configuration; but you can also choose right to left, top to bottom, bottom to top, diagonal, etc.

HALO Graphics functions are also capable of producing detailed hatch patterns for area fills. Personalized hatch patterns can be made up in advance, saved, and called for these fills in any program. There are also functions that address a mouse and allow cursor movement on the screen in response to movement of the mouse. HALO Graphics even accepts input from a number of digitizers and digitizer tablets for finely detailed art work.

While HALO Graphics can drive many different graphics boards, some with resolutions of 1000 by 1000 pixels, the remainder of this discussion assumes the use of the IBM Color Graphics Adapter with two modes of operation:

Medium Resolution: Four colors, 320 by 200 pixels
High Resolution: Monochrome, 640 by 200 pixels

Differences will be noted when other boards provide HALO functions with arguments that go outside the limited screen coordinate and four-color capability of the IBM Color Graphics Adapter, (by todays standards) a fairly limited color board.

USING HALO WITH GCLISP

To use HALO Graphics with GCLISP, you must first purchase the HALO Graphics software designed this language. HALO Graphics is usually available in two major versions. Standard HALO is dedicated to a particular MS-DOS machine, graphics board, printer, etc. The other is MULTIHALO, which contains the drivers for many different type of MS-DOS machines, color cards, printers, locators, etc.

Gold Hill Computers supplies the MULTIHALO version with GCLISP. This is a plus, because it will allow you to address different types of printers, locators, and especially graphics boards. MULTIHALO was used for the graphics portion of this text.

To use HALO functions with GCLISP, first run the HALO driver named HALORGH.EXE *before* entering GCLISP. This file is found on one of the HALO disk. After a few seconds, a prompt will appear telling you that the HALO driver is installed. If you want to use a mouse, you must run another driver before entering GCLISP. This second driver is a, COM file. In researching this book, I used a Mouse Systems mouse whose driver is contained in the HALOMSMI.COM file. Simply type HALOSMI while in DOS and this driver will be installed.

You can also type GCLISP to enter LISP. Load the file called HALOGOLD.LSP. This is done by typing:

```
(LOAD "HALOGOLD.LSP")
```

Next tell HALO what kind of graphics board is installed in your computer. There are device driver files that support the many color boards on the market. These files have a .DEV extension. I used the standard IBM Color Graphics Adapter and its driver is named HALOIBM.DEV. If you have this, you should type:

```
(SETDEV "HALOIBM.DEV")
```

This loads the color card driver. Now you're set to use the graphics functions HALO offers.

Your first HALO Graphics call should be to the IN-ITGRAPHICS function. This initializes the graphics screen to medium-resolution mode when used with an argument of 0 and to high-resolution mode when the argument is 1. These arguments and modes assume the use of the IBM Color Graphics Adapter and correspond with the PC-BASIC SCREEN 1 and SCREEN 2 modes respectively. Once INTERGRAPHICS is called in the format of:

```
(INITGRAPHICS 0)
```

the graphics screen clears. You are now ready to write graphics images to the screen using other HALO functions. The color monitor does not have to be in the default display. If you have both the monochrome display card and the color card, you can default to the monochrome monitor and write graphics to the color monitor.

If you do not want to erase the contents of the color monitor but want to reenter HALO Graphics mode, you can use START-GRAPHICS instead of INITGRAPHICS. STARTGRAPHICS initializes the screen without clearing it.

As mentioned HALO Graphics contains several printer drivers. The driver files have .PRN extensions and support several popular models. I used the IBM dot matrix printer equipped with the graphics option (GRAFTRAX). This is really the EPSON MX-80 printer with IBM's logo on the front. The driver file for this printer is contained on one of the HALO disk and is named HALOEPSN.PRN. Before you can write to the printer, first use the following SETPRN function:

```
(SETPRN "HALOEPSN.PRN")
```

This loads the printer driver. You can dump the entire screen to the printer using (GPRINT) with no arguments.

This short overview of the general initialization procedures for HALO Graphics with GCLISP has focused on IBM. If you are using other color cards, printers, or mice you will have to substitute the appropriate driver files to support them. Your device is probably supported by the many HALO Graphics drivers.

HALO CURSORS

HALO Graphics has three basic cursors: graphics, text, and crosshair cursors. Each cursor marks the point at which a write occurs; however, some functions (such as CIR, which draws a circle) use the cursor as a reference point to perform writes in other areas of the screen.

Graphics Cursor

The graphics cursor is never visible and serves as a reference point for graphics function calls. Several HALO functions are available to move this cursor to the desired screen position. The graphics cursor behaves like the graphics cursor that operates under IBM Advanced BASIC (BASICA). Calling a function that moves the graphics cursor requires arguments that name the X and Y coordinates; even though the cursor moves, there is no on-screen indication, since the graphics cursor is always invisible.

Text Cursor

The HALO text cursor is much like the graphics cursor, but the text cursor names the position where text is to be displayed. HALO text is not similar to standard text. It is a form of graphics that allows what might be called standard text to be enlarged, shrunk, reformatted, etc.

Unlike the graphics cursor, the text cursor can be made visible. Even the size and color of the text cursor can be defined using HALO functions. The text cursor is placed on the monitor screen using the XOR function, that is, the cursor is nondestructive and will not permanently overwrite an image that already exist on the screen, it temporarily covers a portion of the screen image, but when it passes on, this portion is restored.

Crosshair Cursor

The crosshair cursor is the third type of cursor available in HALO graphics. This graphics cursor can also be made visible. It appears as a standard crosshair (+), whose vertical and horizontal elements can be defied in pixel length and color. The crosshair cursor is also a nondestructive cursor; it is often used as a constant indicator of cursor position with a mouse, digitizer pad, or other type of "aiming" peripheral. Various HALO functions turn this cursor on or off. Thus, the crosshair cursor can be used for initial aiming and then commanded to disappear once the screen write has taken place.

COORDINATE FUNCTIONS

In HALO Graphics, there are several functions that do not perform screen writes of any sort; they merely position the various cursors at physical screen positions specified by the function's arguments. Most HALO function arguments must be integer values. This is not the case when operating in the "window" mode or for a few other functions that are discussed later However, if a function expects one type of argument and receives another, chaos can occur.

All cursor-movement functions require integer arguments when operating in standard mode (nonwindow). This is no problem in LISP if constants are the arguments or if variables have integer values. However, dividing an integer variable or constant with functions that require integer arguments requires that the value returned by the division operation is an integer. The TRUNCATE or ROUND functions in Common LISP are often used with these math function returns to assure an integer value.

The HALO function that moves the graphics cursor is called MOVABS, an acronym for "move cursor absolute." Here is typical LISP call using this function:

```
(MOVABS 160 100)
```

The number 160 is the X-coordinate value in pixels and 100 is the Y-coordinate value. This call effectively positions the graphics cursor at the center of the medium-resolution screen.

Another function that specifies coordinates for the graphics cursor is MOVREL, an acronym for "move cursor relative." This means relative to the current position of the graphics cursor on the screen. For instance:

```
(MOVABS 160 100)
(MOVREL 10 0)
```

The first call moves the graphics cursor to screen position 160,100 absolute. The next call uses MOVREL to move the graphics cursor to the X-coordinate of 170. If the first argument to MOVREL were -10, then the new horizontal position would be 150. In this example, the call to MOVREL is the same as saying, "Move the graphics cursor 10 more pixels to the right." The cursor's vertical position remains unchanged, because the Y-coordinate value used with MOVREL is 0. The final graphics cursor position after calling MOVREL is 170, 100.

The text cursor is also moved with parallel functions:

```
MOVTCURABS
```

and

```
MOVTCURREL
```

The first function moves the text cursor to the absolute position named by the function's arguments while the second function moves the text cursor relative to the cursor's position.

Parallel functions for the crosshair cursor are:

```
MOVHCURABS
```

and

```
MOVHCURREL
```

128

You must create both the text and crosshair cursors before making calls that position them. Functions that do this are discussed a bit later.

The cursor position functions are unique entities. They have no equivalents in MS-BASIC, where graphics functions position and write at the same time. For example:

```
10 CIRCLE (160,100),60,1
```

positions the graphics cursor at coordinates 160,100 and then writes a circle on the screen with the circle's center at this point. With HALO Graphics, we must first position the cursor using one function and then write the circle using another.

COLOR

Using the IBM graphics card, we can display up to four different colors at one time on the medium-resolution screen. The colors include three foreground colors and one background color. High-resolution mode supports only one foreground and one background color. The IBM board can also access two palettes of colors; these palettes determine which foreground colors can be accessed.

HALO Graphics offers several functions from which to select palettes, foreground, and background colors. There are also functions that indicate which palette is in use and determine the color of a pixel at any specified point on the screen.

The SETCOLOR function establishes the current foreground write color. In the previous BASIC example using CIRCLE, the function did three things. First, it moved the graphics cursor to the center of the screen. It then selected a foreground color by its color index (the last argument of the BASICA CIRCLE function), which was 1. Last, it wrote a circle in this color at the specified screen coordinates. These same actions require three different function call, in HALO Graphics. First, MOVABS is called to set the graphics cursor to coordinates 160,100. Then the function SET-COLOR is called. SETCOLOR is used with the argument that specifies the color index (1). Next a function is called that writes a circle to the screen.

This may sound like a rather round about way of writing to the screen, but the primitive nature of the functions used to write the circle provides almost unlimited versatility. Moreover, with DEFUN we can easily set up a function that is an exact copy of the BASIC function CIRCLE.

WRITING TO THE SCREEN

Most HALO functions that deal with circles and arcs require a separate function call to position the cursor on the screen *before* conducting a write. However, other functions that write to the graphics screen may contain their own coordinate placement functions.

PTABS/PTREL

The most primitive HALO write function is PTABS, which roughly corresponds with the Advanced BASIC PSET statement. PTABS is used with this format:

```
(PTABS X Y)
```

where X and Y symbolize the X-and Y-coordinates of the screen. PTABS writes a single pixel to the screen at these coordinates. The color value of the pixel is the default color (index 3) unless a call has been made to SETCOLOR specifying another color index. Unlike PSET, which can be used with the format:

```
10 PSET(X,Y),C
```

where C is the desired color index, PTABS only provides the ability to write a pixel in the current screen foreground color at the coordinates specified as PTABS' argument.

This cursor's self-contained move ability is quite handy. If the function were even more primitive, it would simply write a pixel at the current graphics cursor position. Each time a pixel was to be written, it would be necessary first to move the graphics cursor to the new pixel position before calling the pixel write function.

PTABS actually goes through this process, first calling MOVABS before performing a screen write. PTABS calls MOVABS automatically; PTABS is therefore a self-contained function that writes a pixel in the current foreground color at the coordinates specified in its two arguments.

PTABS is an acronym for *point-absolute*. The coordinates provided with PTABS specify the absolute point at which the pixel is to be written. For instance:

```
(PTABS 160 100)
```

writes a pixel in current foreground color at the center of the medium-resolution screen. There is a similar function called PTREL, which stands for *point-relative*. This function makes an automatic call to MOVREL and writes a pixel at coordinates relative to the current position of the graphics cursor. Assuming that the graphics cursor has screen coordinates 160,100, the following call:

```
(PTREL 10 5)
```

writes a pixel at absolute screen coordinates 170,105, which are derived from 160# + #10 and 100# + #5. The pixel color is the screen foreground color, which is a default index of 3-or any value from 0 to 3 if SETCOLOR was called prior to calling a function that writes to the screen.

LNABS/LNREL

Two other HALO functions place a line of pixels between a starting point marked by one set of coordinates and an ending point marked by another coordinate set. These functions are similar to the LINE statement in IBM Advanced BASIC.

LNABS (for line-absolute) draws a line from the current graphics cursor position to a point specified by a single set of coordinates listed in LNABS's arguments.

LNREL (for *line-relative*) also draws a line from the current graphics cursor position, but its arguments specify an offset from this position. Both line functions require MOVABS (or MOVREL) to set an initial starting point for the line.

To draw a line from the upper left-hand corner of the medium-resolution screen to the center of the screen, use both MOVABS and LNABS:

```
(MOVABS 0 0)
(LNABS 160 100)
```

The BASIC equivalent is:

```
10 LINE (0,0)-(160,100)
```

As with PTABS and PTREL, we cannot specify the line's color with the LNABS function. All screen write color specifications must be handled with a prior call to SETCOLOR.

We can write another line from the center of the screen to the upper right-hand corner by using PTREL. This assumes that we drew the first line to the center of the screen (see the above example using LNABS) and that the current position of the graphics cursor is already at screen center (160,100):

```
(PTREL 159 -100)
```

The ending coordinates for the line are 319,0, which are derived from 160 + 159, and 100 – 100.

We can draw this same line using LNABS as in:

```
(LNABS 319 0)
```

Again, this assumes that the graphics cursor is at the center of the screen before this call is made. LNABS and LNREL always write from the position of the graphics cursor. LNABS uses an argument that states the absolute coordinates of the line end point. LNREL uses arguments that specify the X-and Y-coordinate offsets from the current graphics cursor position.

In BASICA, the LINE statement can also be used with the "b" and "bf" arguments (these stand for box and boxfill). This does not hold true for LNABS and LNREL in HALO Graphics. HALO does offer separate functions that write boxes and filled boxes.

Drawing a Box

The BOX function draws a box on the screen much like the BASIC LINE statement does with the "bf" option. BOX uses two sets of absolute coordinates. These specify the upper left-hand and lower right-hand corners of the box. This format is identical to the LINE statement format in BASIC. The following GCLISP call creates an unfilled box in the upper-left quadrant of the medium-resolution graphics screen:

```
(BOX 0 0 160 100)
```

The upper left-hand corner of the box is located at coordinates 0,0, while the lower right-hand corner ends at coordinates 160,000.

If we were to write the same box using LNABS, the program would appear as follows:

```
(MOVABS 0 0)
(LNABS 160 0)
(LNABS 160 100)
(LNABS 0 100)
(LNABS 0 0)
```

MOVABS positions the graphics cursor at coordinates 0,0. The first call to LNABS writes a line at the top of the screen from 0,0 to 160,0. The second call writes from 160,0 to 160,100; the third call from 160,000 to 0,100. The final call completes the box by writing a line from 0,100 to the starting coordinates of 0,0.

The same box can be drawn using LNREL:

```
(MOVABS 0 0)
(LNREL 160 0)
(LNREL 0 100)
(LNREL -160 0)
(LNREL 0 -100)
```

This program specifies the coordinates of each write as an offset to the current graphics cursor position. The changes with each call to LNREL. The first call writes a line from 0,0 to 0 + 160, 0 + 0, which puts the new graphics cursor position at the end of this newly written line (160,0). This next call to LNREL writes a line from 160,0 to 0 + 160, 0 + 100. The cursor position after this write is 160,100. This process continues until the final line in the box attaches to the starting coordinates of 0,0.

The HALO BOX function writes an unfilled box. For a filled box, use the HALO BAR function. This function uses two sets of absolute coordinate arguments that specify the top left-hand and lower right-hand corners of the bar. This is exactly the same coordinate system used with the BOX function. The form written to the screen is a bar or filled box.

Box BOX and BAR write in the current screen's foreground color. If you want to draw a box in one color and fill it with another color, the BAR will not do, because its sides and center will be all the same color. However, you can use BOX and, once the figure is drawn, call other functions that fill enclosed forms with various colors. These latter functions are similar to the PAINT statement in BASICA and are discussed later.

CIR

Circles are written in HALO Graphics using the CIR function. CIR requires only one argument, which specifies CIR's radius in pixels. The center of the circle is the current graphics cursor position. The circle is written in the active screen's foreground color.

The following BASIC program produces a circle at the center of the medium-resolution screen. Its radius is 60-pixels long and its color is represented by the index 3 (white):

```
10 CIRCLE(160,100),60,3
```

This single statement positions the cursor at the center of the screen, sets the color at index 3, and then writes the circle with a radius of 60 pixels.

You must call a number of functions to accomplish the same thing in HALO Graphics:

```
(MOVABS 160 100)
(SETCOLOR 3)
(CIR 60)
```

First, the graphics cursor must be positioned using MOVABS. Then SETCOLOR sets the foreground color. Finally, the circle is written by calling CIR with an argument of 60 for the circle's radius.

If you plan to draw a lot of circles using GCLISP and HALO Graphics, you should write a circle function (assuming you want a function that closely emulates the BASIC CIRCLE statement):

```
(DEFUN CIRCLE (X Y R C)
 (MOVABS X Y)
 (SETCOLOR C)
 (CIR R))
```

There you have it. You can use this function like the BASIC CIRCLE statement; for example:

```
(CIRCLE 160 100 60 3)
```

This very simple function assumes that all values passed to it are integers. Most functions in HALO Graphics take a very dim view of floating-point values. Using them probably won't cause a crash, but the image you are trying to draw won't be produced either. Unless otherwise notes, all arguments to HALO functions must be integers. This means either integer constants or variables that represent integer values. There are some exceptions to this, and there is also a special windowing mode that requires single-precision floating-point arguments for *all* HALO functions. For now, however, remember that most HALO functions in most programming modes need and expect integer arguments. The exceptions are covered a bit later in this chapter.

FILL FUNCTIONS

BASICA's only fill function is called PAINT. HALO Graphics offers three fill functions: FILL, FLOOD, and FLOOD2. Each uses an argument that specifies the color index for the fill. Each can also fill with a user-defined style or hatch pattern. Like PAINT in BASICA, these three fill functions are used to fill *enclosed* geometric figures. With each function, the current position of the graphics cursor determines the seedpoint for the fill. To draw a circle at the center of the screen in color index 3 and then fill it with color index 2, we write:

```
(MOVABS 160 100)
(SETCOLOR 3)
(CIR 60)
(FILL 2)
```

The cursor moves to the center of the screen; SETCOLOR defines the color in which all normal screen writes are produced.

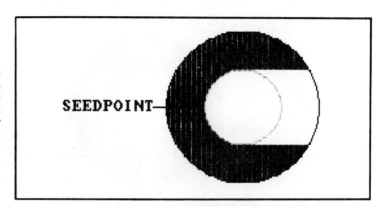

CIR writes the circle and FILL fills that circle with the color represented by index 2 (magenta in palette 1).

FILL is very fast. Unlike PAINT, it doesn't take forever to fill large objects, but there is a catch. FILL can only be used to fill noncomplex shapes such as circles, ellipses, boxes, rectangles, etc. If a form is more complex, FILL can still be used, but you will have to select your seedpoint very carefully (at a point that "looks into" all of the areas to be filled, without rounding corners). Using FILL with forms that are too complex results in an incomplete fill.

In complex cases we can fall back on FLOOD. This function does the same thing as FILL does, but it doesn't work quite so fast and it is not limited by an object's complexity. The screen writes in Figs. 12-1 through 12-3 illustrate the differences between FILL and FLOOD when a complex form is involved.

We want to fill the outer ring of a complex circle that consists of a circle within a circle, each with the same center (i.e., they are concentric circles). Figure 12-1 uses FILL and a seedpoint (cursor location) that falls at the center left of the inner circle. The result is an incomplete fill, the "shaded" opposite side of the outer ring is not filled.

Figure 12-2 also uses FILL, but the seedpoint has been moved

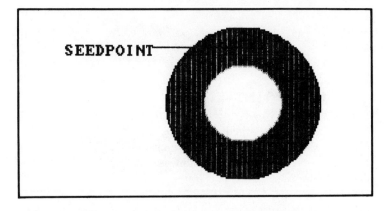

SEEDPOINT

Fig. 12-3. The FLOOD statement, though slower than FILL, is better able to deal with complex shapes.

to the top of the outer ring. This gives too much fill and shades in the entire area. Figure 12-3 uses FLOOD. While FLOOD is much slower than FILL (but far faster than PAINT running under interpretive BASIC), it fills complex shapes without difficulty. FLOOD gives us what we want.

The moral to this demonstration is this: Use FILL for very simple shapes and use FLOOD to fill complex shapes.

FLOOD2 is similar to FLOOD except it can be used to clear out previous fills to shapes. FLOOD2 can overwrite hatch patterns and the like while preserving the shape of the original, unfilled image.

FILL and FLOOD use a single color-index argument that specifies the color of the fill. Unlike PAINT, these functions do not require (and cannot use) the index of the surrounding shape. The seedpoint lies at the current position of the graphics cursor.

TEXT MODES

HALO Graphics offers three modes of text manipulation. One of these, FAST TEXT, is similar to the test-printing statements in MS-BASIC. The FAST TEXT function set includes FTLOCATE, which imitates the LOCATE statement in MS-BASIC. FTEXT, followed by a quoted string or variable, takes the place of the PRINT statement. The FAST TEXT functions allows the mixing of graphics images and standard text on the same graphics screen.

Technically, FAST TEXT does not print standard text; this is done in graphics mode, but the results look the same as standard text. Of course, since FAST TEXT is handled through point graphics, you can alter the text is six and color.

The second mode is GRAPHIC TEXT. It allows the first 127 ASCII characters to be displayed in user-defined heights, widths, colors, and orientations. Orientation can be from left to right, right to left, top to bottom, and bottom to top, to name a few. The position of GRAPHIC TEXT characters is specified by X-and Y-coordinate pairs (as opposed to positioning by character with FTLOCATE). A special GRAPHIC TEXT cursor must be defined; it is usually visible and is manipulated with MOVTCURABS and MOVTCURREL.

The third text mode is STROKE TEXT. This mode provides multiple font types; the other two use the standard IBM text set, which can then be enlarged, widened, shrunk, etc. With STROKE TEXT, the user can define an entire character set that might include cursive characters, Roman numerals, and Greek symbols. The attributes of these fonts are contained in font files that are called by certain HALO STROKE TEXT functions. The HALO package includes several font files and the more experienced user can build others.

We will demonstrate later the different types of text printing available through HALO Graphics. Without these text functions, it would not be possible to mix text and graphics on the same screen.

INQUIRE FUNCTIONS

The HALO functions discussed so far either move the cursor or write pixels to the graphics screen. It is also necessary to read information from the screen. A good example of this is the POINT function in BASICA. POINT returns the color index of the pixel located at the coordinates that serve as POINT's arguments. For example:

```
10 C=POINT(160,100)
```

This operation assigns C the color index of the pixel located at screen coordinates 160,100.

HALO Graphics has several functions that return values based on information present on the screen. These are called the INQUIRE functions and the first part of the name of each of these functions begins with INQ. Any HALO function beginning with INQ will return a value instead of writing something to the screen.

The HALO Graphics equivalent of the PAINT function is called INQCLR, an acronym for *inquire-color*. Its format is:

```
(INQCLR X Y C)
```

X and Y represent the screen coordinates of the pixel to be read and C is the variable that will hold the return color index. Note that this format can be quite misleading when HALO Graphics functions are called from GCLISP. In other languages, the above example works find. Variables X and Y contain the screen coordinates of the pixel to read. Variable C is an integer type and, following the call to INQCLR, would be equal to the color index of the pixel.

But GCLISP passes integer arguments quite differently from other languages and special processing is required to obtain what we want. The object in this example is to assign C the color index of the pixel at coordinates X and Y. Here's how we accomplish this:

```
(SETF X 160 Y 100)
(INQCLR X Y 0)
(SETF C (AREF HALO-LIST 2)
```

HALO functions that return values always return them to the global array named HALO-LIST. This array contains all arguments passed to the *last* HALO function called. After the call to INQCLR, the first three elements of HALO-LIST will be equal to 160,100, and the color index value, respectively. The array element list starts with element zero. Therefore:

```
HALO-LIST0 = 160
HALO-LIST1 = 100
HALO-LIST2 = Color Index
```

We access the elements of HALO-LIST using the Common LISP function AREF (discussed in an earlier chapter). INQCLR contains three arguments. The first two name the screen coordinates. The third is a dummy argument of zero. (The value is unimportant as long as it is an integer constant. It could have been a variable previously assigned an integer value.) Again, this is a dummy argument that does nothing more than fulfill INQCLR's need for three arguments.

After it is called, INQCLR returns its arguments to HALO-LIST. Now the third argument is no longer a dummy. It is equal to the color index of the pixel located at the coordinates supplied by the first two arguments. SETF assigns C the value of the third element in HALO-LIST. Remember, the array element are counted from zero. The first element is therefore at position 0, the second at position 1, and the third at position 2. Position 2 is accessed by AREF; this returns the value of the third INQCLR argument to be assigned to variable C.

This is a pain in the neck. However, Common LISP is quite versatile and allows us to define our own functions. The following function uses INQCLR for an easier implementation of this useful graphics tool:

```
(DEFUN GETCLR (X Y)
  (INQCLR X Y 0)
  (AREF HALO-LIST 2))
```

The new function is called GETCLR and it requires only two arguments that represent the screen coordinates. Within the function body, INQCLR is called with the same arguments as GETCLR, plus the zero dummy argument. Then AREF accesses the desired element of HALO-LIST. The end result is a function that directly returns the color index of the pixel at the screen coordinates.

With such a function we can now write:

```
(SETF C (GETCLR 160 100))
```

Variable C will be equal to the color index of the desired pixel.

There are some INQUIRE functions that always return single-precision floating-point values. One is INQASP, which returns the aspect ratio of the screen. This is the relationship of horizontal pixels to vertical pixels. The ratio defaults to 1.0 in medium-resolution mode, but it can be changed using the HALO function SETASP.

I always use SETASP at the beginning of a graphics routine to change this default ratio to 0.8. This makes perfectly round circles using the IBM Color Graphics Adapter and the Princeton Graphic Systems HX-12 RGB color monitor.

SETASP always requires a floating-point value as its argument. Thus:

```
(SETASP .8)
```

performs the aspect reset procedure.

Some programs may change aspect many times to bring about a desired effect. It is often necessary to change the aspect based upon its current value. This is where INQASP comes in. It returns the current screen aspect ratio as a single-precision floating-point value. We can go to the HALO-LIST array for this valve as we did with INQCLR, but this is not necessary for floating-point values in GCLISP. Floating-point returns from HALO functions can be passed directly to variables in GCLISP. The following example shows how INQASP assigns the current screen aspect-ratio to variable A:

```
(SETF A 0.0)
(INQASP A)
```

Variable A is first set to a dummy value. Notice that this value is in single-precision floating-point form. Don't use an integer constant here or you'll get an error. Also, don't try to use double-precision floating-point values. These won't work either. If variables representing either integers of double-precision numbers must be supplied as arguments, then use the COERCE function to convert them to single-precision values.

The above example assigns A the ratio of the screen. This can be confirmed by simply typing the symbol A with no surrounding parentheses; A evaluates to the aspect ratio.

There are many other INQUIRE functions that return the background color, FAST TEXT cursor positions, graphics cursor position, etc., but these are not discussed in this overview.

OF MICE AND LISP

HALO Graphics supports several locator devices, including the mouse. At present, mice made by Mouse Systems, Summagraphics, and Microsoft are directly supported. Other types may also work if they are compatible with any one of these mice.

To initialize a mouse, use the SETLOCATOR function with the format:

(SETLOCATOR *device port*)

DEVICE is a number that identifies the type of mouse you are using. A chart is provided that matches the numbers with the three compatible mice. The PORT value names the serial port to which the mouse is connected; it is either 1 or 2 on the standard IBM PC.

As soon as SETLOCATOR has been called, the system constantly read the mouse. The return values from the mouse are read by the READLOCATOR function, which works like the INQUIRE functions. READLOCATOR has this format:

```
(READLOCATOR X Y SW)
```

X and Y are variables that hold the X-and Y-coordinates returned, and SW is a variable that holds the current configuration of the mouse buttons. READLOCATOR returns all of these values.

In normal mode, all of these values are integers. It is therefore necessary to go to the array HALO-LIST to retrieve these values. The following is a very basic mouse routine:

```
(SETLOCATOR 1 1)
(READLOCATOR 0 0 0)
(AREF HALO-LIST 0)
(AREF HALO-LIST 1)
(AREF HALO-LIST 2)
```

This example first initializes the mouse. The arguments used with SETLOCATOR identify the Mouse Systems mouse (code 1) and COM1: (the latter is the first serial port). READLOCATOR is then called with three *integer* dummy arguments of 0. Next, the program calls AREF three times, accessing the first three elements of the HALO-LIST array.

Now let's define a function that will allow the mouse to move a visible crosshair cursor on the graphics screen:

```
(DEFUN MOUSER ()
  (SETLOCATOR 1 1)
  (INITHCUR 10 10 3)
  (LOOP (READLOCATOR 0 0 0)
        (SETF X (AREF HALO-LIST 0))
        (SETF Y (AREF HALO-LIST 1))
        (MOVHCURABS X Y)))
```

MOUSER is the name of this function and it is called without arguments. SETLOCATOR initializes for the Mouse Systems mouse and names port 1. These arguments will be different if you are using another brand of mouse and another serial port. Next, INITHCUR is called and it initializes a visible crosshair cursor. The visible cursor consists of vertical and horizontal elements that are each 10 pixels long. The color of these lines is index 3 (white).

The Common LISP LOOP function is used to create an endless loop. This function has not been discussed, because it is very primitive and many advocates of Common LISP feel that it will be modified in future versions. In any event, it accepts multiple arguments and continues executing until an exit sequence is evaluated. The arguments to LOOP in this example do not include an exit sequence, so an endless loop is created. (This loop also could have been accomplished with DO.)

Within the endless loop, READLOCATOR reads the mouse coordinates. Next, SETF assigns X and Y the returned values of the mouse from HALO-LIST. These values then serve as arguments to MOVHCURABS, which positions the crosshair cursor at the mouse coordinates. The end result is a crosshair cursor that moves *with* the movement of the mouse.

A more complex program might also read the switch positions from the third element in HALO-LIST (position number 2). This later return would allow other HALO functions to draw circles, boxes, lines, etc., at the point referenced by the mouse.

RUBBERBAND FUNCTIONS

A rubberband function writes an image that looks like it is made of rubber because its position or dimensions change in a smooth, elastic manner. The Apple Macintosh and its MacPaint program popularized rubberband graphics; now you can have the same graphics ability with HALO Graphics.

Rubberband functions work nicely with mouse control. The functions work by animation routines. A rubberband line is simply a standard line that is written to the screen. However, when the rubberband line function is called again, the old rubberband line disappears and the new one is written, presumably in a nearby position. The old line disappears because it is XORed with itself. In animation terminology, XORing an image with itself erases the image completely.

HALO Graphics three principal rubberband functions are RBOX, RCIR, and RLNABS. RLNABS has a relative coordinate counterpart in the form of RLNREL. Each of these functions is called just like their counterparts, BOX, CIR, and LNABS. You can write a normal circle on the screen with:

```
(RCIR 60)
```

It will appear no different than a circle written with:

```
(CIR 60)
```

However, when you make another call to RCIR, the first circle disappears. Therefore:

```
(RCIR 60)
(RCIR 30)
```

first writes a circle with a radius of 60 pixels and then erases it and writes another circle with the same center, but this time with a radius of 30 pixels. This occurs rapidly and the circle appears to shrink to half its original size; this is called *rubberbanding*.

If you are writing a program that will allow the user to move to various screen positions with the mouse and then write circles, lines, etc., rubberband functions are what you need. When a rubberband image is to be made permanent, you must use the function's nonrubberband equivalent, such as CIR. In other words, we locate and form the image using, for example, RCIR. Once the circle is the correct size and in the right position, we must delete it and then rewrite it using CIR. It is absolutely essential to delete a rubberband image before rewriting it permanently.

Fortunately there are three matching HALO commands specifically for this purpose. DELBOX, DELCIR, and DELLN are called without arguments to delete a rubberband box, circle, or line, respectively. Remember, there can be only one rubberband image from these three categories on the screen at one time. This limitation occurs automatically, because every time another rubberband function is called, the previous image drawn by the matching rubberband function disappears and is replaced by the most current.

We can use RCIR and the mouse to move a rubberband circle around the screen. When we have the position and circle size we want, the rubberband circle is deleted using DELCIR. CIR is then called with the same radius value that was used with the last rubberband circle. This leaves a permanent circle at our specified location.

The following routine writes a rubberband circle at the center of the medium-resolution screen. The circle will grow very large and then shrink down to nothing before expanding again. This is done by using two loops to set the changing values of the radius argument to RCIR:

```
        (DO  ((X  1  (+  1  X)))
              (NIL)
              (RCIR  X)
              (WHEN  (=  X  101)
  (DO  ((Y  101  (-  Y  1)))
       ((=  Y  1)  (SETF  X  1))
       (RCIR  Y))))
```

This should clearly demonstrate the use of one rubberband function. RBOX and RLNABS work in a similar fashion.

The following program is a very crude drawing too that allows the user to write lines to the screen using RLNABS. It is set up for the Mouse Systems mouse operating from port 1. The crosshair cursor follows the mouse's movements. When you wish to start a line, press the left-hand mouse button once and release it. From this point on, a rubberband line follows the mouse from the point occupied by the crosshair cursor. When you want to "set" the line, simply press the left-hand button again. This causes LNABS to be called and sets the line permanently. The program follows:

```
(INITGRAPHICS  0)
(SETLOCATOR  1  1)
(DO  ((Q  1)))
     (NIL)
     (INITHCUR  5  5  3)
     (READLOCATOR  0  0  0)
     (SETF  X  (AREF  HALO-LIST  0))
     (SETF  Y  (AREF  HALO-LIST  1))
     (SETF  SW  (AREF  HALO-LIST  2))
     (MOVHCURABS  X  Y)
     (WHEN  (=  SW  132)
                    (SETF  A  X  B  Y)
                    (DO  ((R  1)  (C  0))
                         ((=  C  1))
     (READLOCATOR  0  0  0)
     (SETF  X  (AREF  HALO-LIST  0))
     (SETF  Y  (AREF  HALO-LIST  1))
     (SETF  SW  (AREF  HALO-LIST  2))
     (MOVABS  A  B)
```

```
(RLNABS X Y)
(WHEN (= SW 132)
         (SETF C 1)
         (DELLN)
         (MOVABS A B)
         (LNABS X Y)))))))
```

The best way to learn the interconnection between the mouse and rubberband functions in HALO Graphics is to play around with various routines that allow simple writes. The above program is quite simple. It could be made much more efficient (and shorter too), but it is written to emphasize the major steps of its operation.

WORLD COORDINATE MODE

The rule that most HALO functions require integer arguments was watered down many times in this chapter with the cave at that this might not be true in every operating mode. This is the case in world coordinate mode. Functions that require integer arguments will require floating-point arguments when operating in this mode.

World coordinate mode allows us to reassign the minimum and maximum values of the screen. In medium-resolution mode, the IBM PC screen is composed with 320 horizontal pixels and 200 vertical pixels. With HALO Graphics we can rearrange how these pixels are addressed in programming. For instance, we can declare the screen to be a 1000 by 1000 set of points instead of 320 by 200. Calling (MOVABS 999 999) will place a pixel in the lower right-hand corner of the screen. Don't think that world coordinates somehow change the resolution of the screen. That is hardware-controlled and cannot be changed through programming. World coordinates only allow us to turn the screen pixels on and off using a different set of coordinates.

SETWORLD requires arguments that are real numbers. This means single-precision floating-point values, not integers and not double-precision floats. Its format is:

```
(SETWORLD X1 Y1 X2 Y2)
```

where:

X1 = lower left X-coordinate
Y1 = lower left Y-coordinate
X2 = upper right X-coordinate
Y2 = upper right Y-coordinate

These coordinates for the standard IBM PC medium-resolution screen are:

```
X1 = 0
Y1 = 199
X2 = 319
Y2 = 0
```

This tends to be a bit confusing to BASIC programmers who have not taken advantage of the world coordinate mode available in BASICA. Just remember that the coordinates of the world screen are the minimum X-coordinate value, the maximum Y-coordinate value (in this order).

The following demonstration should make world coordinates seem less exotic:

```
(INITGRAPHICS 0)
(SETWORLD 0.0 1000.0 1000.0 0.0)
(MOVABS 500.0 500.0)
(CIR 250.0)
```

This program simply writes a circle at the center of the screen. INITGRAPHICS is called with an argument of 0; this function initializes the medium-resolution graphics screen. SETWORLD establishes a world screen whose left-hand corner coordinates are 0,0 and whose lower right-hand corner coordinates are 1000,1000. Therefore, a call to (MOVABS 500.0 500.0) moves the graphics cursor to the center of the screen. Actual physical screen coordinates are still 160,100, but world coordinate mode specifies the center as 500.0,500.0.

Notice that all HALO functions that move the cursor or write to the screen are handed arguments that are single-precision floats. This is mandatory while programming in world mode. Integers have no effect on the arguments. Other functions, such as those that specify color indices, will still require integer arguments like (SET-COLOR 3) when used in word mode. These function always use interger arguments, regardless of the mode of operation.

Functions that return coordinate values must be handed dummy arguments in floating-point format (i.e., 0.0). READLOCATOR returns coordinate values as well as the switch code. Here it is necessary to supply floating-point dummy arguments for the coordinate return and an integer dummy value for the switch return, the late return always being an integer. For example:

```
(READLOCATOR 0.0 0.0 0)
```

Note that the last argument to READLOCATOR is 0, not 0.0. This last argument is always given in integer format regardless of the mode of programming. The first two arguments will be integers when in normal mode and floats when in world mode.

World coordinates allow graphics programs to be written that are independent of any hardware constraints on actual coordinates. For example, a graphics application that was originally written for a high-resolution screen composed of 1000 × 1000 pixels can run successfully on the standard IBM color screen with its 320 × 200 pixel format through the use of world coordinates. The IBM screen will still have the same resolution, but world coordinates map the cursor location parameters of the program to the lower resolution screen.

THE SETVIEWPORT FUNCTION

SETVIEWPORT creates separate display areas on the screen. Windows can be written to as separate miniscreens. Using world coordinates, we can assign each miniscreen the same set of minimum and maximum screen coordinates as the physical screen.

SETVIEWPORT used this format:

```
(SETVIEWPORT X1 Y1 X2 Y2 B BK)
```

where:

    X1 = upper left X-coordinate
    Y1 = upper left Y-coordinate
    X2 = lower right X-coordinate
    Y2 = lower right Y-coordinate
    B = border color index
    BK = background color index

Note that setviewport's coordinate specification order is *different* from the order use with SETWORLD. With SETVIEWPORT, we specify the upper left-hand X-and Y-coordinates, and then the lower right-hand X-and Y-coordinates. These coordinates are specified as floats, while the two-color index arguments are specified as integers. The border color is the color of the window's frame. The background color is the color of the window itself, or the color of the surface that it will be written on. If the border is value −1, then there is no window border.

The coordinate arguments to SETVIEWPORT are given as fractions of the entire world screen. For example:

```
(SETWORLD 0.0 0.0 0.5 0.5 1 2)
```

initializes a window that is comprised of the upper left-quarter of the physical screen. The upper left-corner of the window is at 0,0, and the lower right-corner is at .5,.5.

A window that fills the entire screen is initialized by:

```
(SETVIEWPORT 0.0 0.0 1.0 1.0 1 2)
```

The minimum argument value for these coordinates is 0.0 and the maximum argument value is 1.0.

In both examples the border color index is set to 1 and the background is set to 3. The colors represented by these indices are used for the border and background of the window, respectively. The following program sets up four windows on the screen and writes and fills a circle in each:

```
(INITGRAPHICS 0)
(SETWORLD 0.0 199.0 319.0 0.0)
(SETVIEWPORT 0.0 0.0 .5 .5 1 0)
(MOVABS 160.0 100.0)
(CIR 80.0)
(FILL 1)
(SETVIEWPORT .5 0.0 1.0 .5 2 0)
(MOVABS 160.0 100.0)
(CIR 60.0)
(FILL 2)
(SETVIEWPORT 0.0 .5 .5 1.0 3 0)
(MOVABS 160.0 100.0)
(CIR 50.0)
(FILL 3)
(SETVIEWPORT .5 .5 1.0 1.0 1 0)
(MOVABS 160.0 100.0)
(CIR 40.0)
(FILL 1)
(WORLDOFF)
(CLOSEGRAPHICS)
```

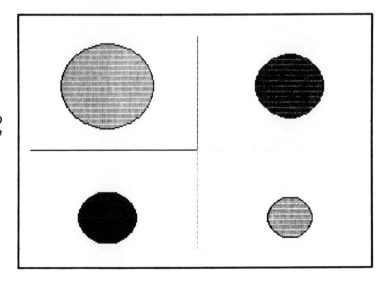

Fig. 12-4. Four windows of the HALO Graphics screen, with a filled circle drawn in each.

Figure 12-4 shows the screen write that divides the screen into 4 windows. In each window a circle is written and filled using the CIR and FILL functions.

SUMMARY

This discussion merely touches on HALO Graphics. GCLISP is a very powerful programming package and HALO Graphics uses this power for graphics and text representation. Remember that HALO Graphics is a set of graphics tools separate from Common LISP. However, these tools are called from within the LISP environment, so they are interfaced with a LISP program. HALO Graphics is similar to a programming language, but it needs an active language environment in which to work. By combining an active language environment in which to work. By combining the power of GCLISP and the graphics power of HALO, programmers will be able to address a full range of artificial intelligence problems.

Appendix

Appendix

Appendix:

GCLISP Windows

GCLISP has numerous functions that allow the windowing of text in selected portions of the screen. In GCLISP, a window is a type of input/output stream that produces and receives characters in a more or less exclusive manner from the remainder of the screen.

MAKE-WINDOW-STREAM

The function MAKE-WINDOW-STREAM creates a window stream. It sets up the window using parameters for height, width, top position, left position, page, etc. When this function is used with SETF, a symbol can represent this window-stream configuration for fast access to different windows all over the screen. Functions can be defined with DEFUN, which causes a screen to activate and display information.

MAKE-WINDOW-STREAM's form is:

```
(MAKE-WINDOW-STREAM :KEYWORD
:KEYWORD
:KEYWORD .....)
```

the keywords are:

```
:HEIGHT
:WIDTH
:TOP
```

```
:LEFT
:STATUS
:PAGE
:CURSORPOS-X
:CURSORPOS-Y
:ATTRIBUTE
```

MAKE-WINDOW-STREAM uses each of these as an argument with values that represent each entity. Defaults are in effect if all keywords are not used, so all keywords usually do not have to be assigned. A description of the keywords follows:

:HEIGHT □ Sets the initial height of the window, measured in lines. Its value must be an integer between 1 and 25. The default value is 24.

:WIDTH □ Sets the initial window width, measured in columns. Its value is an integer in the range from 3 to 80. The default is 80.

:TOP □ Sets the initial offset in lines from the top of the physical display to the top line of the window. This value must be an integer in the range from 0 to 24. The default is set at an offset of 0.

:LEFT □ Sets the initial offset in columns from the left-most column of the physical display to the left-most column of the window. This value must be an integer in the range of 0 to 79. The default is 0.

:STATUS □ Sets certain behavioral attributes of the window based on the value of a bit vector represented by the values 0, 2, 4, or 6. The default is 4. Bit 1 determines whether a physical cursor will appear in the window. Bit 1 also determines whether window text lines are scrolled or wrapped. Bit 2 determines whether a new line is automatically inserted at column end.

:PAGE □ Sets the display page on which the window will be displayed. The default is 0 and the value must be an integer in the range of 0 to 3.

:CURSORPOS-X □ Sets the initial cursor offset in columns from the left-most column of the window. Default is 0 offset; this value must be an integer between 0 and 79.

CURSORPOS-Y □ Sets the initial offset in lines of the cursor from the top of the window; it must be an integer in the range of 0 to 24. The default is 0.

:ATTRIBUTE □ Sets the display attributes of the characters displayed in the window. This value must be an unsigned integer (positive integer) in the range of 0 to 65535.

Note: The :PAGE and :ATTRIBUTE keyword arguments are IBM PC-dependent. :PAGE has meaning only when using the Color/Graphics Monitor Adapter. :PAGE is ignored when using the Monochrome Display Adapter.

A WINDOW EXAMPLE

This example of MAKE-WINDOW establishes a window at the top left-corner of the display screen that is 15 columns wide and 15 lines high. SETF allows a symbol to represent the window:

```
(SETF LISP-WINDOW
      (MAKE-WINDOW-STREAM
                          :WIDTH 15
                          :HEIGHT 15))
```

This may seem simpler than the keyword discussion would lead you to believe, but this example uses the many default values that automatically place the window in the upper left-hand corner of the screen. If the window were to be located at the bottom right of the screen, then it would be necessary to include :TOP and :LEFT. These keywords would have values like 15 and 60, respectively. This would place the left-hand top corner of the window 15 lines from the top of the screen and 60 columns to the right of the left side of the screen. Offset from the right side would be 19 columns.

WRITING TO THE WINDOW

Once the window has been created, you can direct text to it. All LISP operations must be sent to the window using the SEND function. SEND's format is:

(SEND *<window- name>* :*keyword/arguments*)

The symbol LISP-WINDOW (introduced at the beginning of the preceding section) represents the newly created window made with MAKE-WINDOW-STREAM. Briefly, the window operations (keywords) are:

:CLEAR-EOL ☐ Clears characters between the current window cursor position and the end of the line.

:CLEAR-EOS ☐ Clears characters between the current window cursor position and the end of the window.

:CLEAR-SCREEN ☐ Clears the entire window and resets the cursor to position 0,0. (This works like CLS in DOS.)

:INSERT-CHAR ☐ Inserts a space at the current window cursor position and shifts all following characters one place to the right.

154

:INSERT LINES	☐ This keyword is used with an argument that specifies the number of lines to be inserted below the line on which the current window cursor rests.
:DELETE-CHAR	☐ Delectes the character at the current window cursor position. All following characters on the same line are shifted one place to the left.
:DELETE-LINES	☐ This keyword is used with an argument that specifies the number of lines following the one occupied by the cursor that are to be deleted.
:CURSORPOS	☐ Returns the current Cursor position in the format of (X-pos, Y-pos).
:SET-CURSPOS	☐ Sets the window cursor to the position specified by two arguments that name the X- and Y-coordinates.
:POSITION	☐ Returns the offset of the left-most window column from the left-most column of the screen display.
:SET-POSITION	☐ Repositions the window to the position specified by two arguments that name the left and top offsets.
:SIZE	☐ Returns the length and width of the window in lines and columns.
:SET-SIZE	☐ Alters the size of the current window based on two arguments that specify width and height in columns and lines.

:SCROLL

☐ If used without argument, it returns a value that indicates whether the window is currently in scrolling mode. If used with the NIL argument, it sets the window to wrapping mode. With the argument of T it sets the window to scrolling mode.

:AUTO-NEWLINE

☐ If used with no argument, it returns a value indicating whether or not lines that are too long are wrapped. If the argument is NIL, then long lines are automatically wrapped. If T then characters beyond the last column are written in the last column.

:SET-ATTRIBUTE

☐ Used with an integer argument to reset the attributes of the window.

:WRITE-STRING

☐ Used with a string argument to write the contents of the string on the display window, starting at the current window cursor position.

:WRITE-CHAR

☐ Writes the character that serves as its argument to the window at the current cursor position.

:FRESHLINE

☐ Inserts a new line if the cursor is not located at the left-most column position. If it is, then no action takes place.

:CLEAR-INPUT

☐ Clears the input buffer of the window up to the next new line character.

:LISTEN

☐ Returns T if characters are available in the input buffer, NIL if not.

:READ-CHAR	☐ Inputs a character from the keyboard. The character is not echoed to the window.
:READ-CHAR-NO-HANG	☐ Inputs the next character from the buffer if it is immediately available. If not, NIL is returned.
:UNREAD-CHAR	☐ Pushes the most recently read character into the window stream. The new character serves as an argument to this keyword.
:WHICH-OPERATIONS	☐ Returns a list of keywords, defining the window operations that are supported by GCLISP.

Now that we have the essentials, let's write a function that will send characters to the window. The following function named WRITE-WINDOW is defined using DEFUN and uses TEST-WINDOW as the window symbol. TEST-WINDOW was created in a previous example:

```
(DEFUN WRITE-WINDOW ()
  (SEND TEST-WINDOW
  :CLEAR-SCREEN) ;;clears the window
  (SEND TEST-WINDOW
  :WRITE-STRING "WINDOW TEST"))
```

This function clears the windows, and then prints "WINDOW TEXT."

Programming sophisticated "windowing" applications is a task best left to the more experienced programmer. However, many simple applications that utilize windows are within the reach of the Common LISP beginner. With the powerful GCLISP window functions, most of the hard work is done for you. You only have to set up your window and write to the screen with the special window operations that are small in number but large in capability.

Index

Index

READ primitive, 59
    list-building with, 61
READ-CHAR function, 74
READ-LINE function, 74
recursion, 111
REST primitive, 29, 101
REV function, 106
REVERSE function, 107
ROUND function, 128
RPLACA, 35
rubberband function (HALO
    Graphics), 141

S

San Marco LISP Explorer, 4, 7
SECOND primitive, 30, 33
SET, 35
SETF primitive, 24, 33
SETQ, 34
SETVIEWPORT function (HALO
    Graphics), 146
short-float (numeric data subtype),
    98
single-float (numeric data subtype),
    98
Softwriters Inc., 123

special form, 34
Spice LISP, viii
SQRT function, 110
standard-char (character data sub-
    type), 98
STARTGRAPHICS command, 126
Steele, Guy L., Jr., 7
Step (utility), 8
string, Common LISP, 99
string-char (character data subtype),
    98
STRINGP predicate, 56
Symbolics, Inc., 3

T

Tartan Laboratories, Inc., 3
TENP predicate, 54
TERPRI primitive, 67
Texas Instruments, Inc., 3
THIRD primitive, 33
Trace (utility), 8
TRUNCATE function, 128

U

University of California, 3

University of Utah, 3
UNIX, 3
UNLESS conditional, 91

V

VALUES primitive, 48, 90
variable (symbol), 33, 60

W

WHEN conditional, 90
Winston, Patrick H., 7
Wolf, Carl, 118
world coordinates, 144

X

Xerox Corporation, 3

Y

Y-OR-N-P function, 72
Yale University, 3
YES-OR-NO-P function, 73

Z

ZEROP predicate, 54
ZetaLISP, viii, 3

Other Bestsellers From TAB

☐ **THE PERSONAL ROBOT BOOK**

This state-of-the-art "buyer's guide" fills you in on all the details for buying or building your *own and even how to interface a robot with your personal computer!* Illustrated with dozens of actual photographs, it features details on all the newest models now available on the market. Ideal for the hobbyist who wants to get more involved in robotics without getting in over his head. 192 pp., 105 illus. 7″ × 10″.

Paper $12.95   **Hard $21.95**
Book No. 1896

☐ **ROBOTICS—Cardoza and Vlk**

This comprehensive overview traces the historical progression of robotics and the enormous impact robots are making on our society. Includes a look at opportunities and a listing of schools and training programs. Plus, a large comprehensive glossary of robotics terms, a complete bibliography of helpful books, magazines, and information sources, and a listing of the robots now on the market including their manufacturers. 160 pp., 28 illus. 7″ × 10″.

Paper $10.95   **Hard $16.95**
Book No. 1858

☐ **HANDBOOK OF ADVANCED ROBOTICS—Safford**

Here's your key to learning how today's sophisticated robot machines operate, how they are controlled, what they can do, and how you can put this by, and commercial applications. Plus, you'll find complete instructions for building your own remotely available commercial robots and androids; and gain an understanding of the many different types of machines that are classified as robots—including electrically, hydraulically, and pneumatically operated units. 480 pp., 242 illus.

Paper $16.50   **Book No. 1421**

☐ **HOW TO BUILD YOUR OWN SELF-PROGRAMMING ROBOT**

Complete over-the-shoulder instructions on how to use the 8085 microprocessor to build Rodney Robot, a robot capable of thinking and learning. It's a straightforward how-to introduction to the sophisticated subject of robotics and machine intelligence, a practical guide that shows you how to build a robot capable of learning how to adapt to changing circumstances in its environment. 238 pp., 103 illus.

Paper $11.95   **Book No. 1241**

☐ **ARTIFICIAL INTELLIGENCE PROJECTS FOR THE COMMODORE 64™**

This uniquely-exciting guide includes: 16 ready-to-run, fully-explained projects, illustrating a wide variety of artificial intelligence techniques; A plain-English introduction to artificial intelligence, robotics, and LISP; A complete glossary of artificial intelligence terminology; Easy-to-follow examples and show-how illustrations; Plus a quick-look-up index for fast reference. 160 pp., 15 illus. 7″ × 10″.

Paper $12.95   **Book No. 1883**

☐ **ROBOTS AND ROBOTOLOGY—Warring**

Now this exceptional sourcebook can fill you in on what's happening to robot technology from its development to the "intelligent" machines that could someday change the way we live and work. You'll find out how today's sophisticated robots were developed, how they are controlled, and what they can do. Plus, look at 2nd generation industrial robots—that can be programmed to react and analyze data. 128 pp., 82 illus., plus 8-page photo section.

Paper 8.25   **Book No. 1673**

☐ **HOW TO DESIGN AND BUILD YOUR OWN CUSTOM ROBOT—Heiserman**

Now, you can have a robot that "thinks" and "reacts" like you want it to! This incredible, up-to-the-minute sourcebook provides every bit of data you need to make that robot a reality, right in your own home workshop! All the procedures for planning, putting together, and programming a custom-designed parabot, and even an Alpha- or Beta-Class robot are included in this exciting guide to robotics! 462 pp., 247 illus.

Paper $14.95   **Book No. 1341**

☐ **HOW TO BUILD YOUR OWN WORKING ROBOT PET—DaCosta**

An incredible book that shows you how to construct your own microprocessor-based robot and program it—with full details on building an ultrasonic sonar distance measuring navigation system (Soniscan), a hearing method (Excom), a way of talking (Audigen), and an understandable technical/construction data and schematics. 238 pp., 96 illus.

Paper $9.25   **Book No. 1141**